Air Fryer Cookbook for Beginners

2000 Days of Delicious, Quick & Super Easy Air Fryer Recipes for Beginners with a 30-Day Meal Plan and Simple Instructions

Savoring Healthy Living Without Compromising Taste

Julianna Wiggins

Copyright © 2024 By Julianna Wiggins. All rights reserved.

No part of this book may be reproduced, transmitted, or distributed in any form or by any means without permission in writing from the publisher, except in the case of brief quotations embodied in critical articles or reviews.

Legal & Disclaimer

The content and information contained in this book has been compiled from reliable sources, which are accurate based on the knowledge, belief, expertise and information of the Author. The author cannot be held liable for any omissions and/or errors.

TABLE OF CONTENTS

INTRODUCTION...7
CHAPTER 1: UNDERSTANDING YOUR AIR FRYER..8
   Welcome to Air Fryer Cooking... 8
   Getting Started with Your Air Fryer...9
   Essential Air Fryer Tips and Tricks...10
   Maintenance and Cleaning...11
CHAPTER 2: 30-DAY MEAL PLAN..12
CHAPTER 3: QUICK AND HEALTHY BREAKFASTS...16
      Air Fryer Veggie Frittata... 16
      Air Fryer Banana Nut Oatmeal Muffins...16
      Spinach and Feta Air Fryer Omelette..17
      Air Fryer Breakfast Pizza...17
      Air Fryer Veggie Breakfast Tacos...18
      Air Fryer Zucchini and Corn Fritters..18
      Crispy Air Fryer Granola Clusters..19
      Air Fryer Breakfast Sausage Patties...19
      Air Fryer Asparagus and Prosciutto Egg Cups...20
      Air Fryer Berry Breakfast Pitas..20
      Air Fryer Mini Breakfast Quiches...21
      Air Fryer Banana Pepper and Cheese Bagel...21
CHAPTER 4: BREAKFASTS: WEEKEND BRUNCH FAVORITES............................22
   Spiced Apple Air Fryer Turnovers...22
   Air Fryer French Fries..22
   Air Fryer Breakfast Bruschetta...23
   Smoked Salmon and Dill Breakfast Bites...23
   Crispy Air Fryer Hash Browns..24
   Air Fryer Apple Cinnamon Oatmeal Cups..24
   Air Fryer Blueberry Breakfast Scones..25
   Air Fryer Egg and Vegetable Muffins...25
CHAPTER 5: FAMILY BREAKFAST IDEAS..26
   Almond Flour Blueberry Pancakes...26
   Low-Carb Air Fryer Burritos..26
   Coconut-Crusted Banana Slices..27
   Gluten-Free Almond Butter Waffles with Berries..27
CHAPTER 6: LIGHT AND NUTRITIOUS LUNCHES...28
   Air Fryer Mediterranean Chickpea Salad...28
   Air Fryer Quinoa-Stuffed Tomatoes..28
   Air Fryer Cauliflower Steak Pitas..29
   Air Fryer Stuffed Portabello Mushrooms..29
   Air Fryer Asian Style Glazed Eggplant...30

- Air Fryer Buffalo Cauliflower Bites ... 30
- Air Fryer Greek Style Zucchini Fritters ... 31
- Air Fryer Rainbow Veggie Pockets ... 31

CHAPTER 7: WORKDAY MEAL PREP SOLUTIONS ... 32
- Air Fryer Roasted Veggie Quinoa Salad ... 32
- Air Fryer Chicken Fajita Bowls ... 32
- Air Fryer Mini Cheese and Ham Quesadillas ... 33
- Air Fryer Veggie-Stuffed Pita Pockets ... 33
- Air Fryer Herded Pork Tenderloin with Vegetables ... 34
- Crispy Air Fryer Chicken Tenders ... 34
- Air Fryer Spinach and Feta Stuffed Chicken Breasts ... 35
- Air Fryer Caprese Chicken Sandwich ... 35

CHAPTER 8: KID-FRIENDLY LUNCHES ... 36
- Air-Fryer Customizable Pizza ... 36
- Air Fryer Cheese Sticks in Batter ... 36
- Air Fryer Turkey Burger Sliders ... 37
- Air Fryer Rainbow Pizzas ... 37
- Air Fryer Calamari Rings with Garlic Aioli and Mixed Greens ... 38
- Air Fryer Sweet Corn Fritters ... 38
- Chicken Drumsticks in Batter with Honey Mustard Sauce and Fresh Vegetable Salad ... 39
- Air Fryer Turkey and Cheese Roll-Ups ... 39

CHAPTER 9: LUNCH POULTRY AND MEAT RECIPES ... 40
- Turkey and Avocado Air Fryer Wraps ... 40
- Mediterranean Stuffed Bell Peppers ... 40
- Chicken Caesar Salad Pita Pockets ... 41
- Air Fryer Lemon-Herb Chicken Breast with Mixed Vegetables ... 41
- Air Fryer Turkey and Spinach Meatballs ... 42
- Air Fryer Thai Peanut Chicken Lettuce Wraps ... 42
- Air Fryer Pork Steaks with Roasted Broccoli and Carrots ... 43
- Air Fryer Beef Goulash with Vegetables ... 43

CHAPTER 10: HEALTHY SNACK OPTIONS ... 44
- Air Fryer Crispy Chickpea Snack ... 44
- Spiced Butternut Squash Cubes with Walnuts and Cranberries ... 44
- Air Fryer Veggie and Hummus Collard Wraps ... 45
- Air Fryer Zucchini Chips ... 45
- Air Fryer Cumin-Spiced Eggplant Slices with Tahini Sauce ... 46
- Air Fryer Baked Green Pea Fritters ... 46

CHAPTER 11: SNACK PARTY APPETIZERS ... 47
- Air Fryer Broccoli and Cheese Bites ... 47
- Air Fryer Pear and Ginger Crumble ... 47
- Air Fryer Greek Spanakopita Bites ... 48
- Air Fryer Mini Pizza Bites ... 48
- Air Fryer Mini Caprese Skewers ... 49
- Air Fryer Baked Apples with Cinnamon ... 49

CHAPTER 12: SNACK QUICK BITES 50
- Air Fryer Prosciutto-Wrapped Asparagus 50
- Air Fryer Brie and Cranberry Bites 50
- Air Fryer Cucumber and Salmon Canapés 51
- Air Fryer Dark Chocolate Dipped Strawberries 51

CHAPTER 13: SNACK GUILT-FREE DESSERTS 52
- Air Fryer Pear and Granola Parfaits 52
- Air Fryer Matcha Green Tea Mochi 52
- Air Fryer Vegan Chocolate Avocado Cake 53
- Air Fryer Flourless Orange Chocolate Cake 53
- Cinnamon Apple Chips 54
- Air Fryer Honey Glazed Pineapple Slices 54

CHAPTER 14: SNACK BAKED TREATS AND PASTRIES 55
- Air Fryer Gluten-Free Coconut Macaroons 55
- Air Fryer Banana Bread with Almond Flour 55
- Air Fryer Light Angel Food Cake 56
- Air Fryer Lemon and Blueberry Muffins 56

CHAPTER 15: DINNER FISH AND SEAFOOD DELIGHTS 57
- Air Fryer Glazed Mahi Mahi with Mango Salsa and Rice 57
- Asian Style Shrimp and Broccoli 57
- Air Fryer Lemon Herb Tilapia with Quinoa Pilaf 58
- Air Fryer Spicy Tuna Patties 58
- Salmon Steaks with Orange and Soy Glaze, Served with Asparagus 59
- Air Fryer Sweet and Sour Shrimp 59
- Air Fryer Sesame Ginger Salmon Packets 60
- Air Fryer Crispy Tilapia Tacos 60
- Air Fryer Stuffed Calamari with Tomato Sauce 61
- Air Fryer Mini Crab Cakes 61
- Air Fryer Teriyaki Tuna Steaks with Stir-Fried Veggies 62
- Air Fryer Pesto Barramundi with Roasted Cherry Tomatoes 62

CHAPTER 16: FAMILY DINNER FAVORITES 63
- Air Fryer Seafood Paella 63
- Air Fryer Seafood and Asparagus Pasta 63
- Air Fryer Mediterranean Stuffed Sardines 64
- Air Fryer Pasta with Mushrooms and Cheese 64
- Herb-Marinated Anchovies with Roasted Peppers and Baby Greens in Air Fryer 65
- Air Fryer Calamari Rings with Mediterranean Vegetables 65
- Air Fryer Cajun Spiced Catfish with Quinoa Salad 66

CHAPTER 17: DINNER ELEGANT MEALS FOR SPECIAL OCCASIONS 67
- Air Fryer Garlic Shrimp Skewers 67
- Air Fryer Mini Fish Cakes 67
- Air Fryer Herb Crusted Halibut with Lemon Butter Green Beans 68
- Salmon and Asparagus Bundles 68
- Air Fryer Flounder with Spinach and Roasted Cherry Tomatoes 69

Air Fryer Teriyaki Eel Steaks with Stir-Fried Bok Choy... 69
CHAPTER 18: DINNER VEGETARIAN AND VEGAN ADAPTATIONS.. **70**
    Air Fryer Mediterranean Veggie Kebabs... 70
    Crispy Tofu and Broccoli Bowls.. 70
    Air Fryer Thai Red Curry with Vegetables.. 71
    Air Fryer Greek Style Stuffed Eggplant... 71
CHAPTER 19: BONUSES.. **72**
    Meal Plans and Shopping Templates: Tailor-made for Air Fryer Enthusiasts.................................. 72
    Grocery Shopping List for 7-Day Meal Plan... 72
    Grocery Shopping List for 8-14 Day Meal Plan.. 73
    Grocery Shopping List for 15-21 Day Meal Plan.. 74
    Grocery Shopping List for 22-28 Day Meal Plan.. 75

INTRODUCTION

Dear readers,

Welcome to "Air Fryer Cookbook for Beginners", where culinary innovation meets healthy eating. Dive into a world where cooking is no longer a chore but a delightful and healthy journey.

Join Julianna Wiggins, an expert chef with a flair for nutritious cooking, as she guides you through the wonders of air frying. With over ten years in the kitchen, Julianna has perfected the art of making healthy meals that don't skimp on flavor. Her expertise with the air fryer will transform your cooking, making meals quicker, healthier, and more enjoyable.

In this book, Julianna addresses common kitchen woes, from reducing oil in your diet to cooking enjoyable meals quickly. Each chapter is filled with recipes designed to cater to your taste and health needs, making every meal a step towards a healthier lifestyle.

More than just recipes, this book is a lifestyle change. Julianna's approach makes healthy eating effortless, ensuring every dish is a hit with family and friends while boosting your health.

Whether you're a busy parent, a health enthusiast, or just looking to explore new cooking methods, our Air Fryer Cookbook is your ticket to a healthier, happier kitchen experience. Let Julianna Wiggins be your guide on this culinary adventure, turning each page into a step towards better health and delicious meals.

CHAPTER 1: UNDERSTANDING YOUR AIR FRYER

Welcome to Air Fryer Cooking

Congratulations on beginning your journey with one of the most innovative and versatile cooking appliances of our time – the air fryer. This magical device has revolutionized the way we cook, offering a healthier, quicker, and more convenient method to prepare meals that are traditionally fried, baked, or grilled.

The air fryer, in its essence, is a compact convection oven. It uses rapidly circulating hot air combined with a small amount of oil (or sometimes none at all) to cook and crisp food quickly. This method not only reduces the overall calorie and fat content of your meals but also preserves nutrients and flavors, making it an ideal choice for health-conscious food enthusiasts.

Why Air Fryer Cooking?

Air fryer cooking stands out for several reasons:

Health Benefits: By significantly reducing the amount of oil used in traditional frying, air fryers allow you to indulge in your favorite dishes while cutting down on unhealthy fats.

Convenience and Speed: The air fryer heats up quickly and cooks food faster than conventional ovens. It's perfect for busy lifestyles, offering a quick and easy way to prepare meals.

Versatility: From crispy chicken wings and French fries to delicate pastries and roasted vegetables, the range of dishes you can create is vast and varied.

Safety and Cleanliness: With enclosed cooking and minimal oil usage, air fryers are safer and create less mess compared to traditional deep frying.

Energy Efficiency: Air fryers are generally more energy-efficient than ovens, saving you time and reducing utility costs.

Getting to Know Your Air Fryer

Every air fryer model might have its unique features, but most operate on the same basic principles. Here's a quick guide to familiarize you with the essential components:

The Basket: This is where you place the food to be cooked. It's removable for easy cleaning and is usually equipped with a non-stick surface.

The Pan: The basket sits in a pan, which collects any drippings or excess oil from the cooking process.

The Heating Element and Fan: Located at the top of the unit, these work together to circulate hot air around the food, achieving a crispy outer layer while keeping the inside moist.

Temperature and Time Controls: These allow you to adjust cooking settings to suit different recipes.

As we delve deeper into this book, we will explore various recipes and techniques that will turn you into an air fryer pro. Whether you're aiming for crispy fries, juicy meats, or tender vegetables, mastering your air fryer will open up a world of delicious possibilities.

Getting Started with Your Air Fryer

To ensure a smooth start, it's important to understand how to make the most out of your air fryer. Here's a simple guide to help you get started:

1. Unpacking and Initial Setup:

Carefully unbox your air fryer and remove all packaging materials.
Place your air fryer on a flat, heat-resistant surface, ensuring it's not too close to walls or other appliances.
Check for any packaging material or stickers that might be inside the basket or on the heating elements.

2. First-Time Use:

Before cooking food, run your air fryer empty for about 10 minutes at a moderate temperature. This helps to burn off any residues from the manufacturing process and eliminates any plastic-like smells.
After this initial run, let the air fryer cool down, then wipe the basket and pan with a damp cloth to remove any dust or residues.

3. Familiarizing with Controls:

Spend a few minutes getting to know the control panel. Depending on your model, you may have digital controls or analog dials.
Familiarize yourself with setting the temperature and cooking time, and explore any preset cooking functions if available.

4. Understanding Air Fryer Cooking:

The air fryer cooks by circulating hot air around the food. This means food cooks evenly and quickly.
Unlike deep frying, you don't need to submerge food in oil. A light coating of oil, preferably sprayed or brushed, is often enough for most recipes.

5. Cooking Your First Dish:

Start with something simple, like frozen French fries or chicken wings, to get a feel for the cooking process.
Place the food in the basket in a single layer for even cooking. Avoid overcrowding, as this can lead to uneven results.
Halfway through cooking, shake the basket or flip the food to ensure all sides are crispy.

6. Post-Cooking Care:

Always unplug the air fryer and let it cool down before cleaning.
Most air fryers have dishwasher-safe parts, but you can also hand-wash the basket and pan with warm, soapy water.
Wipe down the exterior with a damp cloth and regularly check the heating element for any food residues.

7. Experimenting with Recipes:

Once you're comfortable with the basics, start experimenting with different recipes. You'll find that your air fryer is more versatile than you might have initially thought.

Remember, every air fryer model may vary slightly, so it's a good idea to read through the specific manual for your model. But in general, these tips will set you on the right path to becoming an air fryer expert. Happy cooking!

Essential Air Fryer Tips and Tricks

As you embark on your air fryer cooking journey, a few essential tips and tricks can make your experience smoother, more enjoyable, and yield the best culinary results. Here are some expert recommendations to enhance your air fryer use:

1. Preheating Is Key:

Just like a traditional oven, preheating your air fryer for a few minutes before cooking can lead to better results, especially for foods where you desire a crispy exterior.

2. Avoiding Smoke:

To prevent smoke, especially when cooking fatty foods, add a little water or a piece of bread to the drawer beneath the basket. This will catch dripping fat and reduce smoke production.

3. The Right Amount of Oil:

While air fryers require significantly less oil than traditional frying methods, a light coating of oil can improve both texture and taste. Use an oil spray or a brush to evenly coat your food.

4. Shaking or Flipping for Even Cooking:

For items like fries, vegetables, or small pieces of meat, shake the basket halfway through cooking. This ensures even cooking and browning.

5. Avoid Overcrowding:

Overcrowding the basket can lead to uneven cooking. Cook in batches if necessary to ensure that hot air circulates properly around each piece of food.

6. Using Foil or Parchment Paper:

You can use aluminum foil or parchment paper in the air fryer for easy clean-up. Just ensure that it's weighed down by the food so it doesn't blow into the heating element.

7. Cooking from Frozen:

Air fryers are great for cooking frozen foods. You can cook them directly from frozen, but remember to adjust cooking times accordingly.

8. Baking and Roasting:

Your air fryer isn't just for 'frying.' It's excellent for baking, roasting, and even grilling. Explore recipes beyond fried foods to utilize its full potential.

9. Keep It Clean:

Regular cleaning prevents buildup and smoke and maintains the flavor of your food. Clean the basket and pan after every use.

10. Experiment and Have Fun:

- Don't be afraid to experiment with different recipes. The air fryer's versatility can yield surprising and delightful results.

By following these tips and tricks, you'll not only maximize the lifespan of your air fryer but also enhance your overall cooking experience. Each meal will bring new opportunities to refine your skills and discover the many possibilities that air fryer cooking offers.

Maintenance and Cleaning

Proper maintenance and regular cleaning are crucial for keeping your air fryer in top working condition. Here's a guide to ensure your appliance remains clean, safe, and effective for all your cooking adventures:

1. Daily Cleaning Routine:

After each use, unplug the air fryer and let it cool down completely.
Remove the basket and pan. If they are dishwasher safe, you can place them in the dishwasher for a hassle-free clean. Otherwise, wash them with warm soapy water using a non-abrasive sponge or cloth.
Wipe down the inside of the air fryer with a damp cloth or sponge to remove any food particles or grease. Be careful around the heating element.

2. Deep Cleaning for the Basket and Pan:

For a deeper clean, especially to remove any stuck-on food, soak the basket and pan in hot soapy water for about 10 minutes before washing.
Use a soft-bristled brush to gently scrub away any residue.

3. Cleaning the Exterior:

The exterior of the air fryer should be cleaned regularly with a damp cloth. Avoid using abrasive cleaners or scouring pads, as they can scratch the surface.

4. Handling the Heating Element:

Over time, the heating element can collect grease and food particles. To clean it, first ensure the fryer is unplugged and cool.
Gently brush the heating element with a soft-bristle brush to remove debris. Be cautious not to damage the element.

5. Checking for Wear and Tear:

Regularly inspect the cord, plug, and any other components for signs of wear or damage. If you notice any issues, cease using the appliance and consult the manufacturer for advice or repairs.

6. Avoiding Unpleasant Odors:

To prevent or eliminate odors, you can place a half lemon or some vinegar in the basket and run the air fryer for a few minutes at a low temperature.

7. Storing Your Air Fryer:

Store your air fryer in a clean, dry place. Ensure it's completely cool and clean before storing.
Regular upkeep not only maintains the appliance's efficiency but also ensures that your cooked food always tastes fresh and delicious.

CHAPTER 2: 30-DAY MEAL PLAN

Day	Breakfast	Lunch	Snack	Dinner
Day 1	Air Fryer Veggie Frittata (320 kcal) - p.16	Air Fryer Mediterranean Chickpea Salad (450 kcal) - p.28	Air Fryer Crispy Chickpea Snack (200 kcal) - p.44	Air Fryer Glazed Mahi Mahi with Mango Salsa and Rice (380 kcal) - p.57
Day 2	Spinach and Feta Air Fryer Omelette (350 kcal) - p.17	Air Fryer Quinoa-Stuffed Tomatoes (480 kcal) - p.28	Air Fryer Pear and Ginger Crumble (350 kcal) - p.47	Air Fryer Seafood Paella (350 kcal) - p.63
Day 3	Air Fryer Banana Nut Oatmeal Muffins (380 kcal) - p.16	Air Fryer Cauliflower Steak Pitas (440 kcal) - p.29	Air Fryer Mini Caprese Skewers (220 kcal) - p.49	Air Fryer Mediterranean Stuffed Sardines (380 kcal) - p.64
Day 4	Air Fryer Breakfast Pizza (380 kcal) - p.17	Air Fryer Stuffed Portabello Mushrooms (450 kcal) - p.29	Air Fryer Baked Apples with Cinnamon (220 kcal) - p.49	Air Fryer Herb Crusted Halibut with Lemon Butter Green Beans (350 kcal) - p.68
Day 5	Air Fryer Mini Breakfast Quiches (300 kcal) - p.21	Air Fryer Asian Style Glazed Eggplant (420 kcal) - p.30	Air Fryer Zucchini Chips (200 kcal) - p.45	Air Fryer Flounder with Spinach and Roasted Cherry Tomatoes (380 kcal) - p.69
Day 6	Almond Flour Blueberry Pancakes (380 kcal) - p.26	Air Fryer Buffalo Cauliflower Bites (460 kcal) - p.30	Air Fryer Dark Chocolate Dipped Strawberries (200 kcal) - p.51	Asian Style Shrimp and Broccoli (360 kcal) - p.57
Day 7	Gluten-Free Almond Butter Waffles with Berries (350 kcal) - p.27	Air Fryer Greek Style Zucchini Fritters (450 kcal) - p.31	Air Fryer Vegan Chocolate Avocado Cake (220 kcal) - p.53	Air Fryer Lemon Herb Tilapia with Quinoa Pilaf (350 kcal) - p.58
Day 8	Air Fryer Breakfast Bruschetta (340 kcal) - p.23	Air Fryer Roasted Veggie Quinoa Salad (450 kcal) - p.32	Air Fryer Gluten-Free Coconut Macaroons (300 kcal) - p.55	Air Fryer Spicy Tuna Patties (400 kcal) - p.58
Day 9	Smoked Salmon and Dill Breakfast Bites (360 kcal) - p.23	Air Fryer Chicken Fajita Bowls (440 kcal) - p.32	Air Fryer Matcha Green Tea Mochi (200 kcal) - p.52	Air Fryer Sweet and Sour Shrimp 440 kcal) - p.59
Day 10	Crispy Air Fryer Hash Browns (360 kcal) - p.24	Air Fryer Mini Cheese and Ham Quesadillas (460 kcal) - p.33	Cinnamon Apple Chips (200 kcal) - p.54	Salmon Steaks with Orange and Soy Glaze, Served with Asparagus (350 kcal) - p.59
Day 11	Air Fryer Blueberry Breakfast Scones (310 kcal) - p.25	Air Fryer Veggie-Stuffed Pita Pockets (470 kcal) - p.33	Air Fryer Honey Glazed Pineapple Slices (280 kcal) - p.54	Air Fryer Sesame Ginger Salmon Packets (380 kcal) - p.60
Day 12	Air Fryer Apple Cinnamon Oatmeal Cups (380 kcal) - p.24	Air Fryer Pork Steaks with Roasted Broccoli and Carrots (490 kcal) - p.43	Air Fryer Banana Bread with Almond Flour (210 kcal) - p.55	Air Fryer Stuffed Calamari with Tomato Sauce (350 kcal) - p.61
Day 13	Spiced Apple Air Fryer Turnovers (300 kcal) - p.22	Air Fryer Beef Goulash with Vegetables (400 kcal) - p.43	Air Fryer Light Angel Food Cake (210 kcal) - p.56	Air Fryer Mini Crab Cakes (420 kcal) - p.61

Day	Breakfast	Lunch	Snack	Dinner
Day 14	Air Fryer Berry Breakfast Pitas (350 kcal) - p.21	Turkey and Avocado Air Fryer Wraps (460 kcal) - p.40	Air Fryer Lemon and Blueberry Muffins (280 kcal) - p.56	Air Fryer Teriyaki Tuna Steaks with Stir-Fried Veggies (350 kcal) - p.62
Day 15	Air Fryer Breakfast Sausage Patties (320 kcal) - p.19	Chicken Caesar Salad Pita Pockets (470 kcal) - p.41	Air Fryer Gluten-Free Coconut Macaroons (300 kcal) - p.55	Air Fryer Pesto Barramundi with Roasted Cherry Tomatoes (350 kcal) - p.62
Day 16	Air Fryer Asparagus and Prosciutto Egg Cups (360 kcal) - p.20	Air Fryer Lemon-Herb Chicken Breast with Vegetables (450 kcal) - p.41	Air Fryer Matcha Green Tea Mochi (200 kcal) - p.52	Air Fryer Seafood and Asparagus Pasta (400 kcal) - p.63
Day 17	Air Fryer Egg and Vegetable Muffins (360 kcal) - p.25	Air Fryer Thai Peanut Chicken Lettuce Wraps (490 kcal) - p.42	Air Fryer Vegan Chocolate Avocado Cake (200 kcal) - p.53	Herb-Marinated Anchovies with Roasted Peppers and Baby Greens (350 kcal) - p.65
Day 18	Air Fryer Banana Pepper and Cheese Bagel (320 kcal) - p.21	Mediterranean Stuffed Bell Peppers (400 kcal) - p.40	Air Fryer Brie and Cranberry Bites (290 kcal) - p.50	Air Fryer Calamari Rings with Mediterranean Vegetables (350 kcal) - p.65
Day 19	Air Fryer Mini Breakfast Quiches (360 kcal) - p.21	Air Fryer Turkey and Spinach Meatballs (410 kcal) - p.42	Air Fryer Cucumber and Salmon Canapés (300 kcal) - p.51	Air Fryer Cajun Spiced Catfish with Quinoa Salad (350 kcal) - p.66
Day 20	Air Fryer Zucchini and Corn Fritters (370 kcal) - p.18	Air Fryer Pork Steaks with Roasted Broccoli and Carrots (420 kcal) - p.43	Air Fryer Pear and Granola Parfaits (250 kcal) - p.52	Air Fryer Garlic Shrimp Skewers (390 kcal) - p.67
Day 21	Air Fryer Veggie Breakfast Tacos (380 kcal) - p.18	Air Fryer Rainbow Veggie Pockets (430 kcal) - p.31	Air Fryer Dark Chocolate Dipped Strawberries (220 kcal) - p.51	Air Fryer Mini Fish Cakes (440 kcal) - p.67
Day 22	Crispy Air Fryer Granola Clusters (350 kcal) - p.19	Air Fryer Herded Pork Tenderloin with Vegetables (440 kcal) - p.34	Air Fryer Flourless Orange Chocolate Cake (280 kcal) - p.53	Air Fryer Herb Crusted Halibut with Lemon Butter Green Beans (350 kcal) - p.68
Day 23	Spinach and Feta Air Fryer Omelette (350 kcal) - p.17	Air Fryer Chicken Fajita Bowls (450 kcal) - p.32	Air Fryer Baked Green Pea Fritters (200 kcal) - p.46	Salmon and Asparagus Bundles (460 kcal) - p.68
Day 24	Air Fryer Banana Nut Oatmeal Muffins (380 kcal) - p.16	Air Fryer Mini Cheese and Ham Quesadillas (460 kcal) - p.33	Air Fryer Cumin-Spiced Eggplant Slices with Tahini Sauce (200 kcal) - p.46	Air Fryer Flounder with Spinach and Roasted Cherry Tomatoes (380 kcal) - p.69
Day 25	Air Fryer Breakfast Pizza (380 kcal) - p.17	Air Fryer Veggie-Stuffed Pita Pockets (470 kcal) - p.33	Air Fryer Baked Apples with Cinnamon (220 kcal) - p.49	Air Fryer Teriyaki Eel Steaks with Stir-Fried Bok Choy (350 kcal) - p.69

Day	Breakfast	Lunch	Snack	Dinner
Day 26	Air Fryer Veggie Frittata (320 kcal) - p.16	Air Fryer Rainbow Veggie Pockets (480 kcal) - p.31	Prosciutto-Wrapped Asparagus (240 kcal) - p.50	Air Fryer Mediterranean Veggie Kebabs (320 kcal) - p.70
Day 27	Air Fryer Mini Breakfast Quiches (340 kcal) - p.21	Air Fryer Beef Goulash with Vegetables (490 kcal) - p.43	Air Fryer Brie and Cranberry Bites (290 kcal) - p.50	Crispy Tofu and Broccoli Bowls (390 kcal) - p.70
Day 28	Low-Carb Air Fryer Burritos (350 kcal) - p.26	Turkey and Avocado Air Fryer Wraps (400 kcal) - p.40	Air Fryer Cucumber and Salmon Canapés (300 kcal) - p.51	Air Fryer Thai Red Curry with Vegetables (420 kcal) - p.71
Day 29	Air Fryer Asparagus and Prosciutto Egg Cups (360 kcal) - p.20	Chicken Caesar Salad Pita Pockets (410 kcal) - p.41	Air Fryer Veggie and Hummus Collard Wraps (180 kcal) - p.45	Air Fryer Greek Style Stuffed Eggplant (360 kcal) - p.71
Day 30	Coconut-Crusted Banana Slices (350 kcal) - p.27	Air Fryer Lemon-Herb Chicken Breast with Vegetables (450 kcal) - p.41	Air Fryer Zucchini Chips (200 kcal) - p.45	Air Fryer Mediterranean Stuffed Sardines (380 kcal) - p.64

Note: We wish to remind you that the 30-Day Meal Plan provided in this book is intended as a guide and a source of inspiration. The caloric content of the dishes is approximate and may vary depending on the portion sizes and specific ingredients. Our meal plan is designed to provide a diverse and balanced menu, rich in proteins, healthy fats, and carbohydrates. This allows you to maintain a healthy eating without sacrificing the joy of enjoying delicious meals every day.

If you find that the calories in the recipes do not completely align with your personal needs or the plan, feel free to adjust the portion sizes. Increase or decrease them to ensure that the meal plan suits your individual goals and preferences. Be creative and enjoy each dish according to your needs!

CHAPTER 3: QUICK AND HEALTHY BREAKFASTS

Air Fryer Veggie Frittata

Prep: 15 minutes | Cook: 20 minutes | Serves: 4

Ingredients:

- 6 eggs (330g)
- 1/2 cup milk (120ml)
- 1 cup chopped vegetables (bell peppers, onions, spinach) (150g)
- 1/2 cup shredded cheese (50g)
- 1 tbsp olive oil (15ml)
- Salt and pepper to taste

Instructions:

1. In a bowl, whisk together eggs, milk, salt, and pepper.
2. Stir in chopped vegetables and cheese.
3. Grease an air fryer-safe pan with olive oil.
4. Pour the egg mixture into the pan.
5. Cook in the Air Fryer at 360°F (180°C) for 15–20 minutes or until set.

Nutrition Facts (Per Serving): Calories: 220 | Fat: 15g | Carbohydrates: 6g | Protein: 13g | Fiber: 1g

Air Fryer Banana Nut Oatmeal Muffins

Prep: 10 minutes | Cook: 15 minutes | Serves: 6

Ingredients:

- 2 ripe bananas, mashed (200g)
- 1 cup rolled oats (90g)
- 2 eggs (110g)
- 1/4 cup chopped nuts (walnuts or pecans) (30g)
- 1/4 cup honey (60ml)
- 1 tsp baking powder
- 1/2 tsp cinnamon
- Pinch of salt

Instructions:

1. In a bowl, combine mashed bananas, oats, eggs, nuts, honey, baking powder, cinnamon, and salt.
2. Fill muffin cups about 3/4 full with the batter.
3. Place the cups in the air fryer basket.
4. Cook at 350°F (175°C) for 15 minutes or until a toothpick comes out clean.

Nutrition Facts (Per Serving): Calories: 190 | Fat: 6g | Carbohydrates: 30g | Protein: 5g | Fiber: 3g

Spinach and Feta Air Fryer Omelette

Prep: 10 minutes | Cook: 8 minutes | Serves: 2

Ingredients:

- 4 eggs (220g)
- 1/2 cup chopped spinach (30g)
- 1/4 cup feta cheese, crumbled (30g)
- 1 tbsp olive oil (15ml)
- Salt and pepper to taste

Instructions:

1. Beat eggs in a bowl with salt and pepper.
2. Stir in spinach and feta cheese.
3. Grease an air fryer-safe pan with olive oil.
4. Pour the egg mixture into the pan.
5. Cook in the Air Fryer at 370°F (188°C) for 8 minutes or until eggs are set.

Nutrition Facts (Per Serving): Calories: 230 | Fat: 18g | Carbohydrates: 2g | Protein: 15g | Fiber: 0.5g

Air Fryer Breakfast Pizza

Prep: 10 minutes | Cook: 8 minutes | Serves: 2

Ingredients:

- 1 pre-made pizza crust (200g)
- 1/2 cup tomato sauce (120ml)
- 1 cup shredded mozzarella cheese (100g)
- 4 eggs (220g)
- 1/2 cup cooked and diced ham (75g)
- Salt and pepper to taste

Instructions:

1. Spread tomato sauce on the pizza crust.
2. Sprinkle half of the mozzarella cheese over the sauce.
3. Crack eggs onto the pizza, and top with diced ham.
4. Sprinkle the remaining cheese over the toppings.
5. Cook in the Air Fryer at 360°F (180°C) for 8 minutes or until the crust is golden and eggs are set.

Nutrition Facts (Per Serving): Calories: 580 | Fat: 26g | Carbohydrates: 52g | Protein: 35g | Fiber: 3g

Air Fryer Veggie Breakfast Tacos

Prep: 15 minutes | Cook: 10 minutes | Serves: 4

Ingredients:

- 4 small flour tortillas (200g)
- 1 cup scrambled eggs (200g)
- 1/2 cup diced bell peppers (75g)
- 1/2 cup diced onions (75g)
- 1/2 cup shredded cheese (50g)
- 1 tbsp olive oil (15ml)
- Salt and pepper to taste

Instructions:

1. Sauté bell peppers and onions with olive oil in 2.
2. the Air Fryer for 5 minutes at 360°F (180°C).
3. Warm tortillas in the Air Fryer for 1 minute.
4. Assemble tacos with scrambled eggs, sautéed veggies, and shredded cheese.
5. Serve immediately.

Nutrition Facts (Per Serving): Calories: 250 | Fat: 12g | Carbohydrates: 22g | Protein: 12g | Fiber: 2g

Air Fryer Zucchini and Corn Fritters

Prep: 20 minutes | Cook: 15 minutes | Serves: 4

Ingredients:

- 2 medium zucchinis, grated (500g)
- 1 cup corn kernels, fresh or frozen (150g)
- 1/2 cup all-purpose flour (60g)
- 2 eggs (110g)
- 1/4 cup grated Parmesan cheese (25g)
- 2 green onions, finely chopped
- 1 tsp baking powder
- 1/2 tsp garlic powder
- Salt and pepper to taste
- Olive oil spray for cooking

Instructions:

1. Squeeze excess moisture from grated zucchini using a clean cloth.
2. In a bowl, mix zucchini, corn, flour, eggs, Parmesan, green onions, baking powder, garlic powder, salt, and pepper until well combined.
3. Preheat the Air Fryer to 360°F (180°C).
4. Form the mixture into small patties and lightly spray with olive oil.
5. Place fritters in the Air Fryer basket in a single layer, and cook for 10-15 minutes, flipping halfway through, until golden and crisp.
6. Serve hot.

Nutrition Facts (Per Serving): Calories: 210 | Fat: 6g | Carbohydrates: 30g | Protein: 10g | Fiber: 4g

Crispy Air Fryer Granola Clusters

Prep: 10 minutes | Cook: 8 minutes | Serves: 6

Ingredients:

- 2 cups rolled oats (180g)
- 1/2 cup chopped nuts (almonds, walnuts) (60g)
- 1/4 cup honey (60ml)
- 2 tbsp coconut oil, melted (30ml)
- 1 tsp vanilla extract
- 1/2 tsp cinnamon
- Pinch of salt

Instructions:

1. In a bowl, mix together oats, nuts, honey,
2. coconut oil, vanilla extract, cinnamon, and salt.
3. Spread the mixture in the Air Fryer basket lined
4. With parchment paper.
5. Cook at 320°F (160°C) for 8 minutes, stirring
6. halfway through, until golden.
7. Let cool to form clusters.

Nutrition Facts (Per Serving): Calories: 250 | Fat: 12g | Carbohydrates: 30g | Protein: 6g | Fiber: 4g

Air Fryer Breakfast Sausage Patties

Prep: 10 minutes | Cook: 10 minutes | Serves: 4

Ingredients:

- 1 lb ground pork (450g)
- 1 tsp sage
- 1 tsp thyme
- 1/2 tsp garlic powder
- 1/2 tsp onion powder
- 1/4 tsp cayenne pepper
- Salt and pepper to taste

Instructions:

1. In a bowl, mix together pork, sage, thyme, garlic
2. Powder, onion powder, cayenne, salt, and pepper.
3. Form into small patties.
4. Cook in the Air Fryer at 360°F (180°C) for 10 minutes, flipping halfway through.
5. Serve hot.

Nutrition Facts (Per Serving): Calories: 300 | Fat: 24g | Carbohydrates: 1g | Protein: 21g | Fiber: 0g

Air Fryer Asparagus and Prosciutto Egg Cups

Prep: 15 minutes | Cook: 8 minutes | Serves: 4

Ingredients:

- 8 asparagus spears, trimmed (80g)
- 4 slices prosciutto (80g)
- 4 eggs (220g)
- Salt and pepper to taste
- Grated Parmesan cheese for garnish (optional)

Instructions:

1. Wrap two asparagus spears with one slice of
2. prosciutto. Repeat for all.
3. Place each wrapped asparagus in an Air Fryer-safe muffin cup.
4. Crack an egg into each cup.
5. Season with salt and pepper.
6. Cook in the Air Fryer at 370°F (188°C) for 8 minutes or until eggs are set to your liking.
7. Garnish with Parmesan cheese if desired.

Nutrition Facts (Per Serving): Calories: 180 | Fat: 12g | Carbohydrates: 1g | Protein: 16g | Fiber: 0.5g

Air Fryer Berry Breakfast Pitas

Prep: 10 minutes | Cook: 5 minutes | Serves: 4

Ingredients:

- 4 pita breads (200g)
- 1 cup mixed berries (blueberries, raspberries) (150g)
- 1/2 cup cream cheese (120g)
- 2 tbsp honey (30ml)
- 1/2 tsp cinnamon

Instructions:

1. Spread cream cheese evenly inside each pita bread.
2. Fill each pita with mixed berries.
3. Drizzle honey over the berries and sprinkle with cinnamon.
4. Cook in the Air Fryer at 350°F (175°C) for 5 minutes or until pitas are crispy.
5. Serve warm.

Nutrition Facts (Per Serving): Calories: 250 | Fat: 8g | Carbohydrates: 38g | Protein: 6g | Fiber: 3g

Air Fryer Mini Breakfast Quiches

Prep: 15 minutes | Cook: 15 minutes | Serves: 6

Ingredients:

- 6 eggs (330g)
- 1/4 cup milk (60ml)
- 1/2 cup shredded cheddar cheese (50g)
- 1/2 cup diced ham (75g)
- 1/4 cup chopped spinach (30g)
- Salt and pepper to taste

Instructions:

1. In a bowl, whisk together eggs, milk, salt, and pepper.
2. Stir in cheese, ham, and spinach.
3. Pour the mixture into greased Air Fryer muffin cups.
4. Cook at 340°F (170°C) for 15 minutes or until the quiches are set.
5. Serve hot.

Nutrition Facts (Per Serving): Calories: 150 | Fat: 10g | Carbohydrates: 2g | Protein: 12g | Fiber: 0.5g

Air Fryer Banana Pepper and Cheese Bagel

Prep: 5 minutes | Cook: 8 minutes | Serves: 2

Ingredients:

- 2 bagels, halved (200g)
- 1/2 cup grated mozzarella cheese (50g)
- 1/4 cup chopped banana peppers (30g)
- 1 tbsp cream cheese (15g)

Instructions:

1. Spread cream cheese on each bagel half.
2. Top with mozzarella cheese and banana peppers.
3. Cook in the Air Fryer at 360°F (180°C) for 8 minutes or until the bagels are toasted and cheese is melted.
4. Serve warm.

Nutrition Facts (Per Serving): Calories: 320 | Fat: 12g | Carbohydrates: 42g | Protein: 15g | Fiber: 2g

CHAPTER 4: BREAKFASTS: WEEKEND BRUNCH FAVORITES

Spiced Apple Air Fryer Turnovers

Prep: 15 minutes | Cook: 10 minutes | Serves: 4

Ingredients:

- 2 apples, peeled and diced (200g)
- 1/4 cup brown sugar (50g)
- 1/2 tsp cinnamon
- 1/4 tsp nutmeg
- 1 package puff pastry, thawed (250g)
- 1 egg, beaten (50g)

Instructions:

1. In a bowl, whisk together eggs, milk, salt, and pepper.
2. Stir in cheese, ham, and spinach.
3. Pour the mixture into greased Air Fryer muffin cups.
4. Cook at 340°F (170°C) for 15 minutes or until the Quiches are set.
5. Serve hot.

Nutrition Facts (Per Serving): Calories: 150 | Fat: 10g | Carbohydrates: 2g | Protein: 12g | Fiber: 0.5g

Air Fryer French Fries

Prep: 15 minutes | Cook: 20 minutes | Serves: 4

Ingredients:

- 4 large russet potatoes (900g)
- 2 tbsp olive oil (30ml)
- 1 tsp salt (5g)
- 1/2 tsp ground black pepper (1g)
- 1/2 tsp garlic powder (1g) (optional)

Instructions:

1. Peel and cut the potatoes into even-sized sticks, approximately 1/4 inch (6mm) thick.
2. Soak the potato sticks in water for at least 30 minutes to remove excess starch.
3. Drain and thoroughly pat dry the potatoes with a kitchen towel or paper towels.
4. Toss the dried potato sticks with olive oil, salt, pepper, and garlic powder if using.
5. Place in the air fryer basket in a single layer, ensuring they aren't overcrowded (work in batches if needed).
6. Air fry at 380°F (190°C) for 20 minutes, shaking the basket every 5 minutes for even cooking.

7. Serve hot and crisp.

Nutrition Facts (Per Serving): Calories: 220 | Fat: 7g | Carbohydrates: 36g | Protein: 4g | Fiber: 3g

Air Fryer Breakfast Bruschetta

Prep: 10 minutes | Cook: 5 minutes | Serves: 4

Ingredients:

- 4 slices sourdough bread (200g)
- 2 tomatoes, diced (200g)
- 1/4 cup chopped basil (10g)
- 2 cloves garlic, minced
- 1 tbsp olive oil (15ml)
- Salt and pepper to taste
- 1/2 cup crumbled feta cheese (50g)

Instructions:

1. In a bowl, mix together tomatoes, basil, garlic, olive oil, salt, and pepper.
2. Place bread slices in the Air Fryer and cook at 360°F (180°C) for 3 minutes or until lightly toasted.
3. Top each slice of toasted bread with tomato mixture and crumbled feta.
4. Serve immediately.

Nutrition Facts (Per Serving): Calories: 250 | Fat: 9g | Carbohydrates: 33g | Protein: 9g | Fiber: 3g

Smoked Salmon and Dill Breakfast Bites

Prep: 10 minutes | Cook: 5 minutes | Serves: 4

Ingredients:

- 4 slices whole-grain bread (120g)
- 4 oz smoked salmon (115g)
- 1/4 cup cream cheese (60g)
- 2 tbsp chopped fresh dill (6g)
- 1 tbsp capers (15g)
- Salt and pepper to taste

Instructions:

1. Toast bread slices in the Air Fryer at 360°F (180°C) for 3 minutes or until crispy.
2. Spread cream cheese evenly on each slice of toast.
3. Top with smoked salmon, dill, and capers.
4. Season with salt and pepper.
5. Cut into bite-sized pieces and serve.

Nutrition Facts (Per Serving): Calories: 180 | Fat: 9g | Carbohydrates: 15g | Protein: 12g | Fiber: 2g

Crispy Air Fryer Hash Browns

Prep: 15 minutes | Cook: 20 minutes | Serves: 4

Ingredients:

- 2 large russet potatoes, grated (600g)
- 1 small onion, grated (100g)
- 2 tbsp all-purpose flour (15g)
- 1 egg (50g)
- Salt and pepper to taste
- Olive oil spray for cooking

Instructions:

1. Squeeze excess moisture from grated potatoes and onion.
2. In a bowl, mix together potatoes, onion, flour, egg, salt, and pepper.
3. Form mixture into patties.
4. Spray each patty lightly with olive oil.
5. Cook in the Air Fryer at 390°F (200°C) for 20 minutes, flipping halfway through, until golden and crispy.
6. Serve hot.

Nutrition Facts (Per Serving): Calories: 180 | Fat: 1g | Carbohydrates: 38g | Protein: 5g | Fiber: 3g

Air Fryer Apple Cinnamon Oatmeal Cups

Prep: 15 minutes | Cook: 15 minutes | Serves: 6

Ingredients:

- 2 cups rolled oats (180g)
- 1 tsp baking powder
- 1/2 tsp cinnamon
- 1/4 tsp salt
- 1 apple, peeled and diced (150g)
- 1/4 cup honey (60ml)
- 1 egg (50g)
- 1 cup milk (240ml)
- 1 tsp vanilla extract

Instructions:

1. In a bowl, combine oats, baking powder, cinnamon, and salt.
2. Stir in diced apple, honey, egg, milk, and vanilla extract.
3. Fill greased muffin cups with oatmeal mixture.
4. Cook in the Air Fryer at 350°F (175°C) for 15 minutes or until set.
5. Serve warm.

Nutrition Facts (Per Serving): Calories: 220 | Fat: 3g | Carbohydrates: 40g | Protein: 7g | Fiber: 4g

Air Fryer Blueberry Breakfast Scones

Prep: 15 minutes | Cook: 12 minutes | Serves: 8

Ingredients:

- 2 cups all-purpose flour (240g)
- 1/3 cup sugar (67g)
- 1 tbsp baking powder
- 1/2 tsp salt
- 1/2 cup unsalted butter, chilled and cubed (115g)
- 3/4 cup heavy cream (180ml)
- 1 cup fresh blueberries (150g)
- 1 egg, beaten (for egg wash) (50g)

Instructions:

1. In a bowl, combine flour, sugar, baking powder, and salt.
2. Cut in butter until mixture resembles coarse crumbs.
3. Gently stir in heavy cream until just combined.
4. Fold in blueberries carefully.
5. On a floured surface, shape the dough into a circle and cut into 8 wedges.
6. Brush each scone with beaten egg.
7. Cook in the Air Fryer at 350°F (175°C) for 12 minutes or until golden brown.
8. Serve warm.

Nutrition Facts (Per Serving): Calories: 310 | Fat: 16g | Carbohydrates: 38g | Protein: 5g | Fiber: 1gg

Air Fryer Egg and Vegetable Muffins

Prep: 15 minutes | Cook: 15 minutes | Serves: 6

Ingredients:

- 6 eggs (330g)
- 1/2 cup diced bell pepper (75g)
- 1/2 cup diced onion (75g)
- 1/2 cup spinach, chopped (30g)
- 1/4 cup milk (60ml)
- Salt and pepper to taste
- Cheese for topping (optional)

Instructions:

1. In a bowl, whisk together eggs, milk, salt, and pepper.
2. Stir in bell pepper, onion, and spinach.
3. Pour the mixture into greased Air Fryer muffin cups.
4. Top with cheese if desired.
5. Cook at 340°F (170°C) for 15 minutes or until the muffins are set.
6. Serve hot.

Nutrition Facts (Per Serving): Calories: 120 | Fat: 7g | Carbohydrates: 3g | Protein: 9g | Fiber: 1g

CHAPTER 5: FAMILY BREAKFAST IDEAS

Almond Flour Blueberry Pancakes

Prep: 10 minutes | Cook: 15 minutes | Serves: 4

Ingredients:

- 1 1/2 cups almond flour (150g)
- 2 eggs (100g)
- 1/2 cup milk (almond or regular) (120ml)
- 1 tbsp honey (15ml)
- 1 tsp baking powder
- 1/2 cup blueberries (75g)
- Pinch of salt
- Butter or oil for cooking

Instructions:

1. In a bowl, mix almond flour, eggs, milk, honey, baking powder, and salt until smooth.
2. Gently fold in blueberries.
3. Heat a non-stick pan or griddle over medium heat and lightly grease with butter or oil.
4. Pour 1/4 cup of batter for each pancake and cook until bubbles form on the surface, then flip and cook until golden.
5. Serve hot.

Nutrition Facts (Per Serving): Calories: 280 | Fat: 22g | Carbohydrates: 14g | Protein: 11g | Fiber: 4g

Low-Carb Air Fryer Burritos

Prep: 20 minutes | Cook: 10 minutes | Serves: 4

Ingredients:

- 4 low-carb tortillas (200g)
- 1 cup cooked and shredded chicken (125g)
- 1/2 cup black beans (100g)
- 1/2 cup grated cheese (cheddar or mozzarella) (50g)
- 1/4 cup salsa (60ml)
- Salt and pepper to taste

Instructions:

1. Mix chicken, black beans, cheese, and salsa. Season with salt and pepper.
2. Divide the mixture among the tortillas, fold tightly to form burritos.
3. Place burritos in the Air Fryer basket.
4. Cook at 370°F (188°C) for 10 minutes, flipping halfway through, until crispy.
5. Serve warm.

Nutrition Facts (Per Serving): Calories: 250 | Fat: 10g | Carbohydrates: 26g | Protein: 20g | Fiber: 8g

Coconut-Crusted Banana Slices

Prep: 10 minutes | Cook: 10 minutes | Serves: 4

Ingredients:

- 2 bananas, sliced (200g)
- 1 egg, beaten (50g)
- 1 cup shredded coconut (80g)
- 1/2 tsp cinnamon

Instructions:

1. Dip banana slices in beaten egg, then coat with shredded coconut mixed with cinnamon.
2. Place banana slices in the Air Fryer basket in a single layer.
3. Cook at 360°F (180°C) for 10 minutes or until coconut is golden and crispy.
4. Serve warm.

Nutrition Facts (Per Serving): Calories: 200 | Fat: 11g | Carbohydrates: 23g | Protein: 3g | Fiber: 4g

Gluten-Free Almond Butter Waffles with Berries

Prep: 10 minutes | Cook: 15 minutes | Serves: 4

Ingredients:

- 1 1/2 cups gluten-free flour (180g)
- 1/4 cup almond butter (60g)
- 2 eggs (100g)
- 1 1/4 cups milk (almond or regular) (300ml)
- 2 tbsp maple syrup (30ml)
- 1 tsp baking powder
- 1/2 tsp vanilla extract
- Pinch of salt
- Mixed berries for topping (strawberries, blueberries) (150g)

Instructions:

1. In a bowl, whisk together flour, almond butter, eggs, milk, maple syrup, baking powder, vanilla extract, and salt until smooth.
2. Heat a waffle iron and pour the batter to cook according to the iron's instructions until golden.
3. Serve waffles topped with mixed berries.

Nutrition Facts (Per Serving): Calories: 350 | Fat: 15g | Carbohydrates: 45g | Protein: 10g | Fiber: 6g

CHAPTER 6: LIGHT AND NUTRITIOUS LUNCHES

Air Fryer Mediterranean Chickpea Salad

Prep: 20 minutes | Cook: 10 minutes | Serves: 4

Ingredients:

- 1 can chickpeas, drained (15 oz or 425g)
- 1 diced cucumber (150g)
- 1 diced bell pepper (120g)
- 1/2 finely chopped red onion (50g)
- 1/4 cup olive oil (60ml)
- Juice of 1 lemon
- 1 tsp dried oregano (5g)
- Salt and pepper to taste
- 1/4 cup crumbled feta cheese (30g)
- 2 tbsp chopped fresh parsley (30ml)

Instructions:

1. Rinse and pat dry the chickpeas. Air fry at 390°F (200°C) for 8-10 minutes until crispy.
2. In a large bowl, combine the air-fried chickpeas with diced cucumber, bell pepper, and red onion.
3. In a small bowl, whisk together olive oil, lemon juice, oregano, salt, and pepper. Pour this dressing over the salad.
4. Toss the salad with crumbled feta cheese and fresh parsley. Serve the salad chilled or at room temperature.

Nutrition Facts (Per Serving): Calories: 220 | Fat: 14g | Carbohydrates: 20g | Protein: 7g | Fiber: 6g

Air Fryer Quinoa-Stuffed Tomatoes

Prep: 15 minutes | Cook: 10 minutes | Serves: 4

Ingredients:

- 4 large tomatoes (400g)
- 1 cup cooked quinoa (185g)
- 1/2 cup feta cheese, crumbled (75g)
- 1/4 cup basil, chopped (10g)
- 2 cloves garlic, minced
- Salt and pepper to taste

Instructions:

1. Cut the tops off tomatoes and scoop out the insides.
2. In a bowl, mix quinoa, feta, basil, garlic, salt, and pepper.
3. Stuff tomatoes with the quinoa mixture.
4. Cook in the Air Fryer at 370°F (188°C) for 10 minutes. Serve warm.

Nutrition Facts (Per Serving): Calories: 180 | Fat: 7g | Carbohydrates: 23g | Protein: 8g | Fiber: 3g

Air Fryer Cauliflower Steak Pitas

Prep: 20 minutes | Cook: 15 minutes | Serves: 4

Ingredients:

- 1 large head cauliflower (600g)
- 2 tbsp olive oil (30ml)
- 1 tsp paprika
- 1/2 tsp garlic powder
- 4 pita breads (200g)
- 1 cup Greek yogurt (240ml)
- 1/2 cucumber, diced (100g)
- Salt and pepper to taste

Instructions:

1. Slice cauliflower into thick steaks.
2. Brush steaks with olive oil, and season with paprika, garlic powder, salt, and pepper.
3. Cook in the Air Fryer at 400°F (200°C) for 15 minutes, flipping halfway through.
4. Warm pita breads in the Air Fryer for 1 minute.
5. Serve cauliflower steaks in pitas with Greek yogurt and diced cucumber.
6. Serve immediately.

Nutrition Facts (Per Serving): Calories: 330 | Fat: 9g | Carbohydrates: 47g | Protein: 15g | Fiber: 6g

Air Fryer Stuffed Portabello Mushrooms

Prep: 15 minutes | Cook: 8 minutes | Serves: 4

Ingredients:

- 4 large Portabello mushrooms, stems removed (400g)
- 1/2 cup cream cheese (120g)
- 1/4 cup grated Parmesan cheese (25g)
- 1/4 cup chopped spinach (30g)
- 2 cloves garlic, minced
- Salt and pepper to taste

Instructions:

1. In a bowl, mix cream cheese, Parmesan, spinach, garlic, salt, and pepper.
2. Stuff each mushroom cap with the mixture.
3. Cook in the Air Fryer at 360°F (180°C) for 8 minutes or until the mushrooms are tender.
4. Serve warm.

Nutrition Facts (Per Serving): Calories: 150 | Fat: 10g | Carbohydrates: 7g | Protein: 6g | Fiber: 2g

Air Fryer Asian Style Glazed Eggplant

Prep: 20 minutes | Cook: 12 minutes | Serves: 4

Ingredients:

- 2 medium eggplants, sliced (600g)
- 2 tbsp soy sauce (30ml)
- 1 tbsp honey (15ml)
- 1 tbsp sesame oil (15ml)
- 1 tsp minced ginger
- 1 clove garlic, minced
- Sesame seeds for garnish
- Chopped green onions for garnish

Instructions:

1. In a bowl, whisk together soy sauce, honey, sesame oil, ginger, and garlic.
2. Brush each eggplant slice with the sauce.
3. Cook in the Air Fryer at 400°F (200°C) for 12 minutes, flipping halfway through.
4. Garnish with sesame seeds and green onions.
5. Serve warm.

Nutrition Facts (Per Serving): Calories: 120 | Fat: 5g | Carbohydrates: 18g | Protein: 3g | Fiber: 6g

Air Fryer Buffalo Cauliflower Bites

Prep: 15 minutes | Cook: 20 minutes | Serves: 4

Ingredients:

- 1 head cauliflower, cut into florets (500g)
- 1/2 cup buffalo sauce (120ml)
- 1 tsp garlic powder
- Salt to taste
- 1 tbsp olive oil (15ml)

Instructions:

1. In a bowl, toss cauliflower florets with olive oil, garlic powder, and salt.
2. Cook in the Air Fryer at 380°F (193°C) for 10 minutes.
3. Remove and toss with buffalo sauce.
4. Return to the Air Fryer and cook for an additional 10 minutes.
5. Serve hot, with ranch or blue cheese dressing if desired

Nutrition Facts (Per Serving): Calories: 100 | Fat: 7g | Carbohydrates: 8g | Protein: 3g | Fiber: 3g

Air Fryer Greek Style Zucchini Fritters

Prep: 20 minutes | Cook: 10 minutes | Serves: 4

Ingredients:

- 3 medium zucchinis, grated (450g)
- 1/2 cup feta cheese, crumbled (75g)
- 1/4 cup all-purpose flour (30g)
- 2 eggs (100g)
- 2 tbsp fresh dill, chopped (6g)
- 1 clove garlic, minced
- Salt and pepper to taste
- Olive oil spray for cooking

Instructions:

1. Squeeze excess moisture out of the grated zucchini with a towel.
2. In a bowl, mix together zucchini, feta cheese, flour, eggs, dill, garlic, salt, and pepper.
3. Form the mixture into small patties.
4. Lightly spray the Air Fryer basket and patties with olive oil.
5. Cook in the Air Fryer at 370°F (188°C) for 10 minutes, flipping halfway through, until golden and crisp.
6. Serve warm with Greek yogurt or tzatziki sauce.

Nutrition Facts (Per Serving): Calories: 150 | Fat: 8g | Carbohydrates: 12g | Protein: 8g | Fiber: 2g

Air Fryer Rainbow Veggie Pockets

Prep: 15 minutes | Cook: 10 minutes | Serves: 4

Ingredients:

- 4 whole wheat pita breads (200g)
- 1/2 cup hummus (120g)
- 1/2 cup bell peppers, thinly sliced (red, yellow, green) (75g)
- 1/4 cup shredded carrots (30g)
- 1/4 cup purple cabbage, shredded (30g)
- 1/4 cup cucumber, thinly sliced (30g)
- Salt and pepper to taste

Instructions:

1. Cut pita breads in half to create pockets.
2. Spread hummus inside each pita pocket.
3. Fill pockets with bell peppers, carrots, cabbage, and cucumber.
4. Season with salt and pepper.
5. Cook in the Air Fryer at 360°F (180°C) for 10 minutes or until the pitas are crispy and warm.
6. Serve immediately.

Nutrition Facts (Per Serving): Calories: 220 | Fat: 6g | Carbohydrates: 35g | Protein: 8g | Fiber: 5g

CHAPTER 7: WORKDAY MEAL PREP SOLUTIONS

Air Fryer Roasted Veggie Quinoa Salad

Prep: 15 minutes | Cook: 20 minutes | Serves: 4

Ingredients:

- 1 cup quinoa, rinsed (170g)
- 2 cups water (480ml)
- 1 red bell pepper, chopped (150g)
- 1 zucchini, chopped (150g)
- 1/4 cup fresh parsley, chopped (15g)
- 1 yellow squash, chopped (150g)
- 1 red onion, chopped (150g)
- 2 tbsp olive oil (30ml)
- Salt and pepper to taste
- 2 tbsp lemon juice (30ml)

Instructions:

1. Cook quinoa in water according to package instructions. Set aside.
2. Toss bell pepper, zucchini, squash, and onion with olive oil, salt, and pepper.
3. Cook in the Air Fryer at 400°F (200°C) for 15 minutes, stirring halfway through.
4. Mix roasted vegetables with cooked quinoa.
5. Add lemon juice and parsley, and toss to combine. Serve warm or at room temperature.

Nutrition Facts (Per Serving): Calories: 280 | Fat: 8g | Carbohydrates: 45g | Protein: 9g | Fiber: 6g

Air Fryer Chicken Fajita Bowls

Prep: 20 minutes | Cook: 20 minutes | Serves: 4

Ingredients:

- 2 boneless, skinless chicken breasts (400g)
- 1 tbsp fajita seasoning (8g)
- 1 red bell pepper, sliced (150g)
- 1 yellow bell pepper, sliced (150g)
- 1 onion, sliced (150g)
- 2 cups cooked rice (370g)
- 1/2 cup black beans, rinsed and drained (90g)
- 1 avocado, sliced (200g)
- Fresh cilantro for garnish

Instructions:

1. Season chicken with fajita seasoning.
2. Cook chicken in the Air Fryer at 370°F (188°C) for 10 minutes per side.
3. Remove chicken and add bell peppers and onion to the Air Fryer. Cook at 370°F (188°C) for 10 minutes.
4. Slice chicken into strips.

5. Assemble bowls with rice, black beans, chicken, roasted peppers and onions, and avocado.
6. Garnish with cilantro. Serve immediately.

Nutrition Facts (Per Serving): Calories: 420 | Fat: 12g | Carbohydrates: 50g | Protein: 27g | Fiber: 8g

Air Fryer Mini Cheese and Ham Quesadillas

Prep: 10 minutes | Cook: 8 minutes | Serves: 4

Ingredients:

- 8 small flour tortillas (240g)
- 1 cup grated cheddar cheese (100g)
- 1/2 cup cooked ham, chopped (75g)

Instructions:

1. Place half of the tortillas on a flat surface Top with cheese and ham.
2. Cover with the remaining tortillas.
3. Cook in the Air Fryer at 360°F (180°C) for 4 minutes per side or until golden brown and cheese is melted.
4. Cut into wedges and serve warm.

Nutrition Facts (Per Serving): Calories: 320 | Fat: 16g | Carbohydrates: 28g | Protein: 16g | Fiber: 2g

Air Fryer Veggie-Stuffed Pita Pockets

Prep: 5 minutes | Cook: 10 minutes | Serves: 4

Ingredients:

- 4 pita breads (200g)
- 1 zucchini, diced (150g)
- 1 bell pepper, diced (150g)
- 1/2 cup cherry tomatoes, halved (100g)
- 1/4 cup feta cheese, crumbled (50g)
- 2 tbsp olive oil (30ml)
- 1 tsp dried oregano
- Salt and pepper to taste

Instructions:

1. In a bowl, mix zucchini, bell pepper, cherry tomatoes, feta cheese, olive oil, oregano, salt, and pepper.
2. Stuff the vegetable mixture into pita breads.
3. Cook in the Air Fryer at 360°F (180°C) for 10 minutes or until the pitas are crispy and warm.
4. Serve immediately.

Nutrition Facts (Per Serving): Calories: 250 | Fat: 9g | Carbohydrates: 35g | Protein: 8g | Fiber: 5g

Air Fryer Herded Pork Tenderloin with Vegetables

Prep: 15 minutes | Cook: 10 minutes | Serves: 4

Ingredients:

- 1 can (400g) chickpeas, drained and rinsed
- 1/2 cup (80g) finely chopped onion
- 2 cloves garlic, minced
- 2 tablespoons chopped fresh parsley
- 1 teaspoon ground cumin
- 1 teaspoon ground coriander
- 1/2 teaspoon salt
- 1/4 teaspoon black pepper
- 2 tablespoons all-purpose flour
- Cooking spray
- 1/2 cup (120ml) tzatziki sauce (store-bought or homemade)
- Pita bread and fresh veggies for serving

Instructions:

1. In a food processor, combine chickpeas, chopped onion, minced garlic, parsley, cumin, coriander, salt, and black pepper.
2. Pulse until the mixture is well combined but still slightly coarse.
3. Transfer the mixture to a bowl and stir in the all-purpose flour to bind the mixture together.
4. Form the mixture into small falafel patties or balls.
5. Preheat your Air Fryer to 370°F (190°C).
6. Lightly coat the falafel with cooking spray and place them in the Air Fryer basket.
7. Cook for 10 minutes, flipping halfway through, until they are golden brown and crispy.
8. Serve the falafel with tzatziki sauce, pita bread, and fresh veggies.

Nutritional Facts (Per Serving): Calories: 220 | Fat: 8g | Carbohydrates: 30g | Protein: 8g | Fiber: 6g

Crispy Air Fryer Chicken Tenders

Prep: 10 minutes | Cook: 15 minutes | Serves: 4

Ingredients:

- 1 teaspoon garlic powder
- 1 teaspoon onion powder
- 1/2 teaspoon paprika
- Salt and pepper to taste
- Cooking spray
- Dipping sauce of your choice
- 1 pound (450g) chicken tenders
- 1 cup (120g) breadcrumbs
- 1/2 cup (60g) grated Parmesan cheese

Instructions:

1. In a shallow bowl, combine breadcrumbs, grated Parmesan cheese, garlic powder, onion powder, paprika, salt, and pepper.
2. Dip each chicken tender into the breadcrumb mixture, pressing gently to adhere the coating.
3. Preheat your Air Fryer to 375°F (190°C).

4. Lightly coat the chicken tenders with cooking spray and place them in the Air Fryer basket in a single layer.
5. Cook for 12-15 minutes, flipping halfway through, until the chicken is crispy and cooked through.
6. Serve with your favorite dipping sauce. Enjoy!

Nutritional Facts (Per Serving): Calories: 280 | Fat: 12g | Carbohydrates: 20g | Protein: 25g | Fiber: 2g

Air Fryer Spinach and Feta Stuffed Chicken Breasts

Prep: 20 minutes | Cook: 25 minutes | Serves: 4

Ingredients:

- 4 chicken breasts (200g each)
- 1 cup chopped fresh spinach (30g)
- 1/2 cup crumbled feta cheese (75g)
- 1 tsp minced garlic (5g)
- Salt and pepper to taste
- 1 tbsp olive oil (15ml)

Instructions:

1. Make a horizontal cut in each chicken breast to create a pocket.
2. In a bowl, mix together the chopped spinach, crumbled feta cheese, minced garlic, and a dash of salt and pepper.
3. Stuff this mixture into the pockets of each chicken breast.
4. Brush the chicken breasts with olive oil and season the outside with salt and pepper.
5. Place the stuffed chicken breasts in the air fryer and cook at 360°F (180°C) for 20-25 minutes, or until the chicken is fully cooked through.

Nutrition Facts (Per Serving): Calories: 270 | Fat: 12g | Carbohydrates: 2g | Protein: 36g | Fiber: 1g

Air Fryer Caprese Chicken Sandwich

Prep: 10 minutes | Cook: 15 minutes | Serves: 4

Ingredients:

- 4 chicken breasts (150g each)
- 1 tsp Italian seasoning (5g)
- Salt and pepper to taste
- 4 slices fresh mozzarella cheese (30g each)
- 1 large tomato, sliced (180g)
- Fresh basil leaves
- 4 whole wheat sandwich buns (50g each)
- 2 tbsp balsamic glaze (30ml)

Instructions:

1. Season chicken breasts with Italian seasoning, salt, and pepper.
2. Place the seasoned chicken in the air fryer and cook at 360°F (180°C) for 10 minutes.
3. Top each chicken breast with a slice of mozzarella cheese and return to the air fryer for an additional 3-5 minutes, or until the cheese is melted and chicken is fully cooked.
4. Toast the sandwich buns in the air fryer for 2 minutes if desired.
5. Assemble the sandwiches by placing the chicken and mozzarella on the buns, followed by tomato slices and fresh basil.
6. Drizzle with balsamic glaze before serving.

Nutrition Facts (Per Serving): Calories: 350 | Fat: 9g | Carbohydrates: 32g | Protein: 38g | Fiber: 3g

CHAPTER 8: KID-FRIENDLY LUNCHES

Air-Fryer Customizable Pizza

Prep: 10 minutes | Cook: 14 minutes | Serves: 2

Ingredients:

- 1 pre-made pizza dough (200g)
- 1/2 cup pizza sauce (120ml)
- 1 1/2 cups shredded mozzarella cheese (150g)
- 1/2 cup mixed bell peppers, sliced (75g)
- 1/2 cup red onions, diced (75g)
- 1/2 cup black olives, sliced (75g)
- 1/2 cup cherry tomatoes, halved (75g)
- 1/2 cup cooked chicken breast, diced (75g)
- 1/2 cup broccoli florets, lightly steamed (75g)
- Fresh basil leaves for garnish
- Olive oil for brushing (15ml)
- Salt and pepper to taste

Instructions:

1. Roll out pizza dough on a floured surface to fit air fryer basket size. Brush one side with olive oil.
2. Preheat air fryer to 360°F (182°C).
3. Transfer dough, oiled side down, into the basket. Air-fry for 3-4 minutes until it starts to brown. Remove and brush the top side with oil.
4. Flip the crust, spread pizza sauce, leaving border. Top with cheese.
5. Add bell peppers, onions, olives, tomatoes, chicken, and broccoli. Season with salt and pepper.
6. Cook in air fryer for 7-10 minutes until cheese melts and vegetables are tender.
7. Cool for a couple of minutes, garnish with basil. Serve with extra sauce if desired.

Nutrition Facts (Per Serving): Calories: 380 | Fat: 15g | Carbohydrates: 40g | Protein: 22g | Fiber: 3g

Air Fryer Cheese Sticks in Batter

Prep: 10 minutes + Freezing | Cook: 8 minutes | Serves: 4

Ingredients:

- 12 mozzarella sticks (10g each)
- 1 cup all-purpose flour (120g)
- Salt and pepper to taste
- 1 egg
- 1 cup breadcrumbs (120g)
- 1 tsp Italian seasoning (3g)

Instructions:

1. Freeze mozzarella sticks for at least 2 hours.
2. Coat each stick in flour, then dip in beaten egg, and finally in breadcrumbs mixed with Italian seasoning, salt, and pepper.

3. Air fry at 400°F (200°C) for 6-8 minutes, until golden and cheese is melted.

Nutrition Facts (Per Serving): Calories: 320 | Fat: 16g | Carbohydrates: 25g | Protein: 18g | Fiber: 2g

Air Fryer Turkey Burger Sliders

Prep: 10 minutes | Cook: 15 minutes | Serves: 4

Ingredients:

- 1 lb ground turkey (450g)
- 1 teaspoon garlic powder (5g)
- 1 teaspoon onion powder (5g)
- Salt and pepper to taste
- 8 slider buns (30g each)
- Lettuce, tomato slices, and condiments for serving

Instructions:

1. Mix ground turkey with garlic powder, onion powder, salt, and pepper.
2. Form into 8 small patties.
3. Cook in air fryer at 360°F for 15 minutes, flipping halfway.
4. Serve on slider buns with lettuce, tomato, and your favorite condiments.

Nutrition Facts (Per Serving): Calories: 280 | Fat: 10g | Carbohydrates: 25g | Protein: 20g | Fiber: 2g

Air Fryer Rainbow Pizzas

Prep: 20 minutes | Cook: 10 minutes | Serves: 4

Ingredients:

- 4 small pre-made pizza crusts (85g each)
- 1/2 cup pizza sauce (125ml)
- 1 cup shredded mozzarella cheese (100g)
- Assorted colored bell peppers, thinly sliced (100g)
- 1/2 red onion, thinly sliced (50g)
- 1/4 cup black olives, sliced (30g)
- Fresh basil leaves for garnish

Instructions:

1. Spread pizza sauce over each crust.
2. Top with mozzarella, bell peppers, red onion, and black olives.
3. Cook in air fryer at 360°F for 10 minutes, until cheese is melted and crust is crisp.
4. Garnish with fresh basil leaves before serving.

Nutrition Facts (Per Serving): Calories: 290 | Fat: 12g | Carbohydrates: 32g | Protein: 12g | Fiber: 3gg

Air Fryer Calamari Rings with Garlic Aioli and Mixed Greens

Prep: 15 minutes | Cook: 10 minutes | Serves: 2

Ingredients:

- 1/2 lb calamari rings (225g)
- 1/2 cup all-purpose flour (60g)
- 1 egg, beaten
- 1 cup panko breadcrumbs (50g)
- 1/2 tsp paprika (1g)
- Salt and pepper to taste
- 1/4 cup mayonnaise (60ml)
- 1 clove garlic, minced (3g)
- 1 tbsp lemon juice (15ml)
- 2 cups mixed greens (lettuce, arugula) (60g)
- 1 tbsp olive oil (15ml)

Instructions:

1. Set up three bowls - one with flour, one with beaten egg, and one with panko mixed with paprika, salt, and pepper.
2. Dredge calamari rings first in flour, then egg, and finally in panko mixture.
3. Air fry calamari at 400°F (204°C) for 10 minutes, flipping halfway, until golden and crispy.
4. Mix mayonnaise, minced garlic, and lemon juice to create garlic aioli.
5. Toss mixed greens in olive oil and a pinch of salt.
6. Serve calamari rings with garlic aioli and a side of mixed greens.

Nutrition Facts (Per Serving): Calories: 400 | Fat: 18g | Carbohydrates: 35g | Protein: 25g | Fiber: 2g

Air Fryer Sweet Corn Fritters

Prep: 15 minutes | Cook: 8 minutes | Serves: 4

Ingredients:

- 2 cups fresh corn kernels (300g)
- 1/2 cup all-purpose flour (60g)
- 1/4 cup cornmeal (40g)
- 1/4 cup milk (60ml)
- 1 large egg
- 2 tbsp chopped green onions (15g)
- 1/4 tsp paprika (1g)
- Salt and pepper to taste
- Cooking spray

Instructions:

1. In a bowl, combine corn, flour, cornmeal, milk, egg, green onions, paprika, salt, and pepper. Mix until well combined.
2. Form into small patties.
3. Spray air fryer basket with cooking spray. Place patties in the basket, and spray tops with cooking spray.
4. Cook in air fryer at 390°F for 8 minutes, flipping halfway through, until golden and crispy.

Nutrition Facts (Per Serving): Calories: 180 | Fat: 3g | Carbohydrates: 33g | Protein: 6g | Fiber: 3g

Chicken Drumsticks in Batter with Honey Mustard Sauce and Fresh Vegetable Salad

Prep: 20 minutes | Cook: 25 minutes | Serves: 4

Ingredients:

For Chicken Drumsticks:
- 8 chicken drumsticks (100g each)
- 1 cup all-purpose flour (120g)
- 1 tsp garlic powder (3g)
- 1/2 tsp paprika (1g)
- 1/2 cup milk (120ml)
- 1 egg
- Salt and pepper to taste

For Honey Mustard Sauce:
- 1/4 cup honey (60ml)
- 1/4 cup Dijon mustard (60ml)
- 1 tbsp apple cider vinegar (15ml)
- Salt and pepper to taste

For Fresh Vegetable Salad:
- 2 cups mixed greens (lettuce, spinach, arugula) (60g)
- 1 cucumber, sliced (150g)
- 1 carrot, julienned (60g)
- 1 bell pepper, sliced (120g)
- 1 tbsp olive oil (15ml)
- 1 tbsp lemon juice (15ml)
- Salt and pepper to taste

Instructions:

For the Chicken Drumsticks:

1. Mix flour, garlic powder, paprika, salt, and pepper in a bowl.
2. Whisk milk and egg in another bowl.
3. Dip each drumstick in the milk mixture, then in the flour mixture.
4. Cook in the air fryer at 375°F (190°C) for 25 minutes, turning halfway through.

For the Honey Mustard Sauce:

1. Whisk together honey, mustard, vinegar, salt, and pepper until smooth.

For the Fresh Vegetable Salad:

1. Toss mixed greens, cucumber, carrot, and bell pepper with olive oil, lemon juice, salt, and pepper.
2. Serve the crispy chicken drumsticks with honey mustard sauce for dipping and a side of fresh vegetable salad.

Nutrition Facts (Per Serving): Calories: 450 | Fat: 15g | Carbohydrates: 40g | Protein: 30g | Fiber: 3g

Air Fryer Turkey and Cheese Roll-Ups

Prep: 5 minutes | Cook: 8 minutes | Serves: 4

Ingredients:

- 8 slices turkey breast (200g)
- 4 slices Swiss cheese, halved (100g)
- 1/4 cup mustard (60ml)
- 8 toothpicks

Instructions:

1. Spread mustard on each slice of turkey. Place half a slice of cheese on each.
2. Roll up and secure with a toothpick.
3. Cook in air fryer at 360°F for 8 minutes, until turkey is heated and cheese is melted.

Nutrition Facts (Per Serving): Calories: 150 | Fat: 8g | Carbohydrates: 4g | Protein: 17g | Fiber: 0g

CHAPTER 9: LUNCH POULTRY AND MEAT RECIPES

Turkey and Avocado Air Fryer Wraps

Prep: 10 minutes | Cook: 5 minutes | Serves: 4

Ingredients:

- 4 large flour tortillas (50g each)
- 8 slices turkey breast (200g)
- 1 avocado, thinly sliced (200g)
- 1 tomato, sliced (100g)
- 1/4 cup Greek yogurt (60ml)
- Salt and pepper to taste
- 1 cup lettuce, shredded (50g)

Instructions:

1. Spread Greek yogurt on each tortilla.
2. Layer turkey slices, avocado, tomato, and lettuce. Season with salt and pepper.
3. Roll up the tortillas tightly and secure with toothpicks.
4. Place in air fryer and cook at 360°F for 5 minutes, until crisp.

Nutrition Facts (Per Serving): Calories: 310 | Fat: 16g | Carbohydrates: 30g | Protein: 12g | Fiber: 4g

Mediterranean Stuffed Bell Peppers

Prep: 25 minutes | Cook: 20 minutes | Serves: 4

Ingredients:

- 4 bell peppers, tops removed and seeded (200g each)
- 1 cup cooked quinoa (170g)
- 1/2 lb ground meat (beef or turkey) (225g)
- 1/2 cup feta cheese, crumbled (75g)
- Salt and pepper
- 1/4 cup olives, chopped (30g)
- 1/4 cup sun-dried tomatoes, chopped (30g)
- 1/4 cup fresh parsley, chopped (15g)
- 2 tbsp olive oil (30ml)
- 1/2 tsp garlic powder

Instructions:

1. Preheat the air fryer to 350°F (177°C).
2. In a skillet, cook the ground meat with garlic powder, salt, and pepper until browned. Drain excess fat.
3. In a bowl, mix cooked quinoa, cooked meat, feta cheese, olives, sun-dried tomatoes, parsley, and 1 tbsp olive oil. Season with salt and pepper.
4. Stuff the mixture into the bell peppers.

5. Brush the outside of the peppers with the remaining olive oil.
6. Place stuffed peppers in the air fryer basket. Cook for 20 minutes, or until the peppers are tender.

Nutrition Facts (Per Serving): Calories: 350 | Fat: 18g | Carbohydrates: 25g | Protein: 20g | Fiber: 6g

Chicken Caesar Salad Pita Pockets

Prep: 15 minutes | Cook: 0 minutes | Serves: 4

Ingredients:

- 2 cups cooked chicken, shredded (300g)
- 1/2 cup Caesar dressing (120ml)
- 4 pita breads, halved (60g each)
- 1 cup romaine lettuce, shredded (50g)
- 1/4 cup Parmesan cheese, shredded (25g)
- 1/2 cup croutons (30g)

Instructions:

1. Mix chicken with Caesar dressing.
2. Open pita halves to create pockets.
3. Fill each pita pocket with chicken mixture, lettuce, Parmesan cheese, and croutons.

Nutrition Facts (Per Serving): Calories: 350 | Fat: 15g | Carbohydrates: 28g | Protein: 25g | Fiber: 2g

Air Fryer Lemon-Herb Chicken Breast with Mixed Vegetables

Prep: 15 minutes | Cook: 20 minutes | Serves: 2

Ingredients:

- 2 chicken breasts, boneless and skinless (200g each)
- Juice and zest of 1 lemon
- 1 tbsp olive oil for chicken (15ml)
- 1 tsp dried oregano (5g)
- 1 tsp dried thyme (5g)
- Salt and pepper
- 2 cups mixed vegetables (broccoli, carrots, bell peppers) (200g)
- 1 tbsp olive oil for vegetables (15ml)
- 1/2 tsp garlic powder (2g)

Instructions:

1. Marinate chicken breasts in lemon juice, zest, 1 tbsp olive oil, oregano, thyme, salt, and pepper for 10 minutes.
2. mixed vegetables with 1 tbsp olive oil, garlic powder, salt, and pepper.
3. Place chicken breasts in the air fryer basket. Surround with seasoned vegetables.
4. Cook at 360°F (182°C) for 20 minutes, flipping chicken halfway through, until chicken is cooked and vegetables are tender.
5. Serve the lemon-herb chicken with a side of roasted mixed vegetables.

Nutrition Facts (Per Serving): Calories: 300 | Fat: 12g | Carbohydrates: 10g | Protein: 40g | Fiber: 3g

Air Fryer Turkey and Spinach Meatballs

Prep: 15 minutes | Cook: 10 minutes | Serves: 4

Ingredients:

- 1 lb ground turkey (450g)
- 1 cup spinach, finely chopped (30g)
- 1/4 cup breadcrumbs (30g)
- 1 egg
- 1 tsp garlic powder (5g)
- Salt and pepper to taste

Instructions:

1. Combine all ingredients in a bowl. Form into small meatballs.
2. Place meatballs in air fryer basket, ensuring they don't touch.
3. Cook at 380°F for 10 minutes, until cooked through.

Nutrition Facts (Per Serving): Calories: 180 | Fat: 9g | Carbohydrates: 5g | Protein: 20g | Fiber: 1g

Air Fryer Thai Peanut Chicken Lettuce Wraps

Prep: 20 minutes | Cook: 15 minutes | Serves: 4

Ingredients:

- 2 chicken breasts, diced (400g)
- 1 tbsp soy sauce (15ml)
- 2 tbsp peanut butter (30ml)
- 1 tsp ginger, minced (5g)
- 1 tbsp honey (15ml)
- 1 tsp chili flakes (5g)
- 1 head of lettuce, leaves separated (200g)
- 1/4 cup peanuts, chopped (30g)
- 1/4 cup cilantro, chopped (15g)

Instructions:

1. Toss chicken with soy sauce, peanut butter, ginger, honey, and chili flakes.
2. Cook in air fryer at 360°F for 15 minutes, until chicken is cooked.
3. Serve chicken in lettuce leaves, topped with peanuts and cilantro.

Nutrition Facts (Per Serving): Calories: 260 | Fat: 14g | Carbohydrates: 10g | Protein: 27g | Fiber: 2g

Air Fryer Pork Steaks with Roasted Broccoli and Carrots

Prep: 10 minutes | Cook: 20 minutes | Serves:4

Ingredients:

- 4 pork steaks (150g each)
- 1 tbsp olive oil (15ml)
- 1 tsp garlic powder (3g)
- 1/2 tsp smoked paprika (1g)
- Salt and pepper to taste
- 2 cups broccoli florets (150g)
- 2 carrots, sliced (100g each)
- 1 tbsp olive oil for vegetables (15ml)
- 1/2 tsp dried thyme (1g)

Instructions:

1. Season pork steaks with garlic powder, smoked paprika, salt, and pepper. Drizzle with 1 tbsp olive oil.
2. Toss broccoli and carrots with 1 tbsp olive oil, thyme, salt, and pepper.
3. Place pork steaks in the air fryer and cook at 380°F (193°C) for 10 minutes.
4. Add vegetables to the air fryer and cook for an additional 10 minutes, until pork is cooked and vegetables are tender.
5. Serve pork steaks with roasted broccoli and carrots.

Nutrition Facts (Per Serving): Calories: 350 | Fat: 18g | Carbohydrates: 12g | Protein: 35g | Fiber: 3g

Air Fryer Beef Goulash with Vegetables

Prep: 15 minutes | Cook: 30 minutes | Serves:4

Ingredients:

- 1 lb beef stew meat, cubed (450g)
- 1 onion, chopped (100g)
- 2 cloves garlic, minced (6g)
- 1 red bell pepper, chopped (120g)
- 1 cup diced tomatoes (240g)
- 2 cups beef broth (480ml)
- 1 tsp paprika (3g)
- 1/2 tsp caraway seeds (1g)
- Salt and pepper to taste
- 2 tbsp olive oil (30ml)

Instructions:

1. In the air fryer, cook onion, garlic, and bell pepper with olive oil at 380°F (193°C) for 5 minutes.
2. Add beef, tomatoes, beef broth, paprika, caraway seeds, salt, and pepper.
3. Cook in the air fryer at 360°F (180°C) for 25 minutes, stirring occasionally, until the beef is tender.
4. Serve the goulash hot.

Nutrition Facts (Per Serving): Calories: 400 | Fat: 20g | Carbohydrates: 15g | Protein: 40g | Fiber: 3g

CHAPTER 10: HEALTHY SNACK OPTIONS

Air Fryer Crispy Chickpea Snack

Prep: 10 minutes | Cook: 15 minutes | Serves: 4

Ingredients:

- 1 can chickpeas (15 oz or 425g), drained and rinsed
- 1 tbsp olive oil (15ml)
- 1/2 tsp salt (3g)
- 1/4 tsp ground black pepper (1g)
- 1/2 tsp smoked paprika (1g)

Instructions:

1. Pat the chickpeas dry with a paper towel and remove any loose skins.
2. In a bowl, toss the chickpeas with olive oil, salt, pepper, and smoked paprika.
3. Place chickpeas in the air fryer basket in a single layer.
4. Air fry at 390°F (200°C) for 15 minutes, shaking halfway through, until crispy.

Nutrition Facts (Per Serving): Calories: 130 | Fat: 4g | Carbohydrates: 18g | Protein: 6g | Fiber: 5g

Spiced Butternut Squash Cubes with Walnuts and Cranberries

Prep: 15 minutes | Cook: 20 minutes | Serves: 4

Ingredients:

- 1 butternut squash, peeled and cubed (500g)
- 1 tbsp olive oil (15ml)
- 1 tsp cinnamon (3g)
- 1/4 tsp nutmeg (1g)
- 1/2 cup walnuts, chopped (58g)
- 1/4 cup dried cranberries (30g)
- Salt to taste

Instructions:

1. In a bowl, mix butternut squash cubes with olive oil, cinnamon, nutmeg, and a pinch of salt.
2. Place the squash in the air fryer basket in a single layer.
3. Air fry at 400°F (200°C) for 20 minutes, shaking halfway through, until tender and golden.
4. In the last 5 minutes of cooking, add the chopped walnuts and dried cranberries to the basket, mixing with the squash.
5. Serve warm as a nutritious and flavorful snack.

Nutrition Facts (Per Serving): Calories: 200 | Fat: 11g | Carbohydrates: 26g | Protein: 3g | Fiber: 4g

Air Fryer Veggie and Hummus Collard Wraps

Prep: 20 minutes | Cook: 10 minutes | Serves: 4

Ingredients:

- 4 large collard greens leaves (200g)
- 1 cup hummus (240g)
- 1 bell pepper, thinly sliced (150g)
- 1 carrot, julienne (100g)
- 1 cucumber, julienne (200g)
- 1/2 red onion, thinly sliced (50g)
- Salt and pepper to taste

Instructions:

1. Lightly cook collard greens in the air fryer at 360°F (180°C) for 2-3 minutes to soften.
2. Spread hummus on each collard leaf, then top with bell pepper, carrot, cucumber, and red onion.
3. Season with salt and pepper.
4. Roll up tightly, cut in half, and serve.

Nutrition Facts (Per Serving): Calories: 180 | Fat: 8g | Carbohydrates: 24g | Protein: 6g | Fiber: 8g

Air Fryer Zucchini Chips

Prep: 10 minutes | Cook: 15 minutes | Serves: 4

Ingredients:

- 2 medium zucchinis, thinly sliced (300g)
- 1 tbsp olive oil (15ml)
- 1/2 tsp salt (2.5g)
- 1/4 cup breadcrumbs (30g)
- 1/4 tsp pepper (1g)
- 1/2 cup grated Parmesan cheese (50g)

For Greek Yogurt Dip:
- 1 cup Greek yogurt (245g)
- 1 tbsp lemon juice (15ml)
- 1 tbsp chopped fresh dill (3g)
- 1 garlic clove, minced (3g)
- Salt and pepper to taste

Instructions:

1. Toss zucchini slices with olive oil, salt, and pepper in a bowl.
2. Mix Parmesan cheese and breadcrumbs in a separate bowl. Dip each zucchini slice in the mixture to coat.
3. Place coated zucchini slices in a single layer in the air fryer basket.
4. Cook at 375°F (190°C) for 10-15 minutes, until crispy and golden.
5. For the dip, combine Greek yogurt, lemon juice, dill, minced garlic, and a pinch of salt and pepper in a bowl.
6. Serve the zucchini chips immediately with the Greek yogurt dip on the side.

Nutrition Facts (Per Serving): Calories: 200 | Fat: 10g | Carbohydrates: 16g | Protein: 12g | Fiber: 2g

Air Fryer Cumin-Spiced Eggplant Slices with Tahini Sauce

Prep: 10 minutes | Cook: 15 minutes | Serves: 4

Ingredients:

- 1 large eggplant, sliced (500g)
- 2 tbsp olive oil (30ml)
- 1 tsp ground cumin (3g)
- 1/2 tsp garlic powder (2g)
- Salt and pepper to taste

For Tahini Sauce:
- 1/4 cup tahini (60ml)
- 2 tbsp lemon juice (30ml)
- 1 garlic clove, minced (3g)
- 2-3 tbsp water (30-45ml), as needed
- Salt to taste

Instructions:

1. In a bowl, mix olive oil, cumin, garlic powder, salt, and pepper. Brush this mixture on both sides of the eggplant slices.
2. Place eggplant slices in the air fryer basket in a single layer.
3. Air fry at 370°F (190°C) for 15 minutes, flipping halfway through, until golden and tender.
4. Meanwhile, for the tahini sauce, whisk together tahini, lemon juice, minced garlic, and salt in a bowl. Gradually add water until the sauce reaches a desirable consistency.
5. Serve the cumin-spiced eggplant slices drizzled with tahini sauce or with the sauce on the side for dipping.

Nutrition Facts (Per Serving): Calories: 200 | Fat: 16g | Carbohydrates: 15g | Protein: 4g | Fiber: 6g

Air Fryer Baked Green Pea Fritters

Prep: 20 minutes | Cook: 15 minutes | Serves: 4

Ingredients:

- 2 cups frozen green peas, thawed (300g)
- 2 large eggs
- 1/4 cup all-purpose flour (30g)
- 1/4 cup grated Parmesan cheese (30g)
- 2 tbsp chopped fresh mint (6g)
- 1/4 tsp garlic powder (1g)
- Salt and pepper to taste
- 1 tbsp olive oil (15ml) for brushing

Instructions:

1. In a food processor, pulse the green peas until coarsely mashed.
2. Transfer to a bowl, and mix in eggs, flour, 3. Parmesan cheese, mint, garlic powder, salt, and pepper to form a batter.
4. Form the batter into small patties.
5. Brush each patty with olive oil and place them in the air fryer basket in a single layer.
6. Air fry at 375°F (190°C) for 15 minutes, flipping halfway through, until golden and crispy.

Nutrition Facts (Per Serving): Calories: 200 | Fat: 8g | Carbohydrates: 21g | Protein: 11g | Fiber: 5g

CHAPTER 11: SNACK PARTY APPETIZERS

Air Fryer Broccoli and Cheese Bites

Prep: 15 minutes | Cook: 10 minutes | Serves: 4

Ingredients:

- 2 cups broccoli florets, finely chopped (200g)
- 1 cup cheddar cheese, shredded (120g)
- 1/2 cup breadcrumbs (60g)
- 1 large egg (50g)
- 1/2 tsp garlic powder (1g)
- Salt and pepper to taste

Instructions:

1. Combine broccoli, cheddar cheese, breadcrumbs, egg, garlic powder, salt, and pepper in a bowl.
2. Form the mixture into small, bite-sized balls.
3. Place the bites in the air fryer basket in a single layer.
4. Cook at 380°F (193°C) for 10 minutes, until golden and crispy.
5. Serve warm.

Nutrition Facts (Per Serving): Calories: 180 | Fat: 10g | Carbohydrates: 12g | Protein: 10g | Fiber: 2g

Air Fryer Pear and Ginger Crumble

Prep: 15 minutes | Cook: 20 minutes | Serves: 4

Ingredients:

- 4 ripe pears, peeled and chopped (600g)
- 1 tbsp fresh ginger, grated (6g)
- 1/2 cup brown sugar (100g)
- 1 tsp cinnamon (2g)
- 1 cup rolled oats (90g)
- 1/2 cup all-purpose flour (60g)
- 1/4 cup unsalted butter, melted (60g)
- 1/4 cup chopped walnuts (30g)

Instructions:

1. Combine pears, ginger, half of the brown sugar, and cinnamon in a bowl.
2. Mix rolled oats, flour, remaining brown sugar, melted butter, and walnuts for the topping.
3. Place pear mixture in the air fryer, top with crumble mixture.
4. Cook at 360°F (182°C) for 20 minutes until golden.
5. Serve warm.

Nutrition Facts (Per Serving): Calories: 350 | Fat: 14g | Carbohydrates: 55g | Protein: 5g | Fiber: 6g

Air Fryer Greek Spanakopita Bites

Prep: 25 minutes | Cook: 8 minutes | Serves: 4

Ingredients:

- 1 cup spinach, chopped (30g)
- 1/2 cup feta cheese, crumbled (75g)
- 1/4 cup ricotta cheese (62g)
- 2 tbsp fresh dill, chopped (6g)
- 1 green onion, finely chopped (15g)
- 1 large egg, beaten (50g)
- 10 sheets fall dough, cut into 4-inch squares (250g)
- Cooking spray

Instructions:

1. Mix spinach, feta, ricotta, dill, green onion, and half the egg.
2. Spoon mixture onto fall squares, fold into triangles, seal with egg.
3. Spray air fryer basket, place bites in a single layer.
4. Cook at 375°F (190°C) for 8 minutes until golden.
5. Serve warm.

Nutrition Facts (Per Serving): Calories: 180 | Fat: 8g | Carbohydrates: 20g | Protein: 7g | Fiber: 1g

Air Fryer Mini Pizza Bites

Prep: 15 minutes | Cook: 10 minutes | Serves:4

Ingredients:

- 1 cup pizza sauce (240g)
- 1 cup mozzarella cheese, shredded (100g)
- 1/2 cup mini pepperoni slices (50g)
- 24 wonton wrappers (120g)
- 1 tsp Italian seasoning (2g)
- Cooking spray

Instructions:

1. Place wonton wrappers in muffin tins to form cups.
2. Add pizza sauce, mozzarella, pepperoni, and sprinkle with Italian seasoning in each cup.
3. Spray lightly with cooking spray.
4. Cook in air fryer at 375°F (190°C) for 10 minutes until crispy.
5. Serve warm.

Nutrition Facts (Per Serving): Calories: 220 | Fat: 10g | Carbohydrates: 22g | Protein: 12g | Fiber: 1g

Air Fryer Mini Caprese Skewers

Prep: 10 minutes | Cook: 2 minutes | Serves: 4

Ingredients:

- 16 cherry tomatoes (200g)
- 16 small mozzarella balls (200g)
- 16 fresh basil leaves
- 2 tbsp balsamic glaze (30ml)
- 1 tbsp olive oil (15ml)
- Salt and pepper to taste

Instructions:

1. Thread a cherry tomato, basil leaf, and mozzarella ball onto each skewer.
2. Drizzle olive oil over the skewers and season with salt and pepper.
3. Place skewers in the air fryer basket.
4. Cook at 360°F (182°C) for 2 minutes.
5. Drizzle balsamic glaze over skewers before serving.

Nutrition Facts (Per Serving): Calories: 150 | Fat: 10g | Carbohydrates: 5g | Protein: 8g | Fiber: 1g

Air Fryer Baked Apples with Cinnamon

Prep: 10 minutes | Cook: 15 minutes | Serves: 4

Ingredients:

- 4 large apples, cored and halved (800g)
- 1/4 cup brown sugar (50g)
- 1 tsp cinnamon (2g)
- 1/4 cup raisins (40g)
- 2 tbsp unsalted butter, cubed (30g)
- 1/4 cup chopped walnuts (30g)

Instructions:

1. Mix brown sugar, cinnamon, walnuts, and raisins in a bowl.
2. Stuff each apple half with the sugar mixture and top with a cube of butter.
3. Place apple halves in the air fryer basket.
4. Cook at 350°F (177°C) for 15 minutes or until apples are tender.
5. Serve warm, optionally with a scoop of vanilla ice cream.

Nutrition Facts (Per Serving): Calories: 220 | Fat: 8g | Carbohydrates: 38g | Protein: 2g | Fiber: 5g

CHAPTER 12: SNACK QUICK BITES

Air Fryer Prosciutto-Wrapped Asparagus

Prep: 10 minutes | **Cook:** 8 minutes | **Serves:** 4

Ingredients:

- 16 asparagus spears, trimmed (200g)
- 8 slices prosciutto, halved lengthwise (120g)
- 1 tbsp olive oil (15ml)
- Salt and pepper to taste

Instructions:

1. Wrap each asparagus spear with a half slice of prosciutto.
2. Drizzle olive oil over wrapped asparagus and season with salt and pepper.
3. Place in the air fryer basket in a single layer.
4. Cook at 400°F (204°C) for 8 minutes, until asparagus is tender and prosciutto is crispy.
5. Serve warm.

Nutrition Facts (Per Serving): Calories: 80 | Fat: 5g | Carbohydrates: 2g | Protein: 6g | Fiber: 1g

Air Fryer Brie and Cranberry Bites

Prep: 15 minutes | **Cook:** 6 minutes | **Serves:** 4

Ingredients:

- 1 sheet puff pastry, thawed (250g)
- 4 oz Brie cheese, cut into small squares (113g)
- 1/4 cup cranberry sauce (60g)
- 1 egg, beaten (for egg wash) (50g)

Instructions:

1. Cut puff pastry into 2-inch squares.
2. Place a piece of Brie and a teaspoon of cranberry sauce on each square.
3. Fold pastry over the filling and seal edges. Brush with beaten egg.
4. Place in the air fryer basket.
5. Cook at 375°F (190°C) for 6 minutes, until golden and puffy.
6. Serve warm.

Nutrition Facts (Per Serving): Calories: 290 | Fat: 18g | Carbohydrates: 24g | Protein: 7g | Fiber: 1g

Air Fryer Cucumber and Salmon Canapés

Prep: 15 minutes | Cook: 5 minutes | Serves: 4

Ingredients:

- 1 cucumber, sliced into rounds (200g)
- 4 oz smoked salmon, cut into small pieces (113g)
- 1/2 cup cream cheese, softened (120g)
- 1 tbsp fresh dill, chopped (3g)
- 1 tsp lemon juice (5ml)
- Salt and pepper to taste

Instructions:

1. Mix cream cheese with dill, lemon juice, salt, and pepper.
2. Spread a small amount of cream cheese mixture on each cucumber slice.
3. Top with a piece of smoked salmon. Place in the air fryer basket.
4. Cook at 350°F (177°C) for 5 minutes, just to warm through.
5. Serve immediately.

Nutrition Facts (Per Serving): Calories: 150 | Fat: 10g | Carbohydrates: 4g | Protein: 10g | Fiber: 1g

Air Fryer Dark Chocolate Dipped Strawberries

Prep: 15 minutes | Cook: 2 minutes | Serves: 4

Ingredients:

- 1 pound fresh strawberries, washed and dried (450g)
- 8 oz dark chocolate, chopped (225g)
- 1 tbsp coconut oil (15ml)
- Optional toppings: chopped nuts, sprinkles, or sea salt

Instructions:

1. Line a tray with parchment paper.
2. In a microwave-safe bowl, combine dark chocolate and coconut oil. Microwave in 30-second intervals, stirring in between, until completely melted.
3. Dip each strawberry into the melted chocolate, covering about half of the strawberry. Optionally, dip into nuts, sprinkles, or sprinkle with sea salt.
4. Place dipped strawberries on the prepared tray.
5. Refrigerate for 10 minutes to set the chocolate.
6. For a warm, slightly soft chocolate coating, place strawberries in the air fryer basket and cook at 360°F (182°C) for 2 minutes.
7. Serve immediately or store in the refrigerator.

Nutrition Facts (Per Serving): Calories: 220 | Fat: 14g | Carbohydrates: 24g | Protein: 3g | Fiber: 4g

CHAPTER 13: SNACK GUILT-FREE DESSERTS

Air Fryer Pear and Granola Parfaits

Prep: 10 minutes | **Cook:** 15 minutes | **Serves:** 4

Ingredients:

- 2 large pears, sliced (500g)
- 2 cups Greek yogurt (480g)
- 1 cup granola (100g)
- 2 tbsp honey (30ml)
- 1/2 tsp cinnamon (1g)

Instructions:

1. Toss pear slices with cinnamon.
2. Place pear slices in the air fryer basket. Cook at 380°F (193°C) for 15 minutes until tender.
3. Layer Greek yogurt, cooked pear slices, and granola in serving glasses.
4. Drizzle with honey.
5. Serve immediately or chilled.

Nutrition Facts (Per Serving): Calories: 250 | Fat: 5g | Carbohydrates: 42g | Protein: 12g | Fiber: 5g

Air Fryer Matcha Green Tea Mochi

Prep: 25 minutes | **Cook:** 8 minutes | **Serves:** 4

Ingredients:

- 1 cup mochiko (sweet rice flour) (120g)
- 1/4 cup sugar (50g)
- 1 tbsp matcha green tea powder (7g)
- 1 cup water (240ml)
- Cornstarch for dusting (as needed)

Instructions:

1. In a bowl, whisk together mochiko, sugar, and matcha powder.
2. Gradually add water, mixing until a smooth batter forms.
3. Pour the batter into a greased, air fryer-safe dish.
4. Air fry at 350°F (175°C) for 8 minutes, or until set.
5. Dust a cutting board with cornstarch. Turn out the cooked mochi onto the board and cut into pieces.
6. Serve the mochi warm or at room temperature.

Nutrition Facts (Per Serving): Calories: 200 | Fat: 1g | Carbohydrates: 45g | Protein: 2g | Fiber: 1g

Air Fryer Vegan Chocolate Avocado Cake

Prep: 15 minutes | Cook: 20 minutes | Serves: 8

Ingredients:

- 1 ripe avocado, mashed (200g)
- 1/4 cup unsweetened cocoa powder (25g)
- 1/2 cup almond flour (50g)
- 1/4 cup maple syrup (60ml)
- 1 tsp baking powder (4g)
- 1/4 tsp salt (1g)
- 1/2 cup almond milk (120ml)
- 1 tsp vanilla extract (5ml)

Instructions:

1. In a bowl, combine mashed avocado, cocoa powder, almond flour, maple syrup, baking powder, and salt.
2. Gradually mix in almond milk and vanilla extract until smooth.
3. Pour the batter into a greased air fryer-safe cake pan.
4. Air fry at 320°F (160°C) for 20 minutes, or until a toothpick inserted comes out clean.
5. Let cool before serving.

Nutrition Facts (Per Serving): Calories: 200 | Fat: 14g | Carbohydrates: 18g | Protein: 4g | Fiber: 5g

Air Fryer Flourless Orange Chocolate Cake

Prep: 20 minutes | Cook: 30 minutes | Serves:8

Ingredients:

- 2 oranges, boiled and pureed (400g)
- 1 cup almond flour (100g)
- 1/2 cup unsweetened cocoa powder (50g)
- 1 tsp vanilla extract (5ml)
- 1 cup granulated sugar (200g)
- 6 eggs
- 1 tsp baking powder (4g)

Instructions:

1. Blend boiled oranges to a puree.
2. In a bowl, mix almond flour, cocoa powder, sugar, and baking powder.
3. Beat in eggs and vanilla extract. Stir in orange puree.
4. Pour into a greased cake pan that fits in the air fryer.
5. Cook at 320°F (160°C) for 30 minutes. Check with a toothpick for doneness.
6. Let cool before serving.

Nutrition Facts (Per Serving): Calories: 280 | Fat: 12g | Carbohydrates: 38g | Protein: 8g | Fiber: 4g

Cinnamon Apple Chips

Prep: 15 minutes | Cook: 15 minutes | Serves: 4

Ingredients:

- 2 apples, thinly sliced (300g)
- 1 tsp cinnamon (2g)
- 1 tbsp sugar (12g)

Instructions:

1. Toss apple slices with cinnamon and sugar.
2. Arrange in a single layer in the air fryer basket.
3. Cook at 350°F (177°C) for 15 minutes, flipping halfway through.
4. Serve once cooled and crispy.

Nutrition Facts (Per Serving): Calories: 60 | Fat: 0g | Carbohydrates: 15g | Protein: 0g | Fiber: 3g

Air Fryer Honey Glazed Pineapple Slices

Prep: 10 minutes | Cook: 10 minutes | Serves: 4

Ingredients:

- 1 pineapple, peeled and sliced (800g)
- 2 tbsp honey (30ml)
- 1 tsp cinnamon (2g)

Instructions:

1. Mix honey and cinnamon in a bowl.
2. Brush pineapple slices with the honey mixture.
3. Place in the air fryer basket in a single layer.
4. Cook at 380°F (193°C) for 10 minutes, flipping halfway through.
5. Serve warm.

Nutrition Facts (Per Serving): Calories: 140 | Fat: 0g | Carbohydrates: 36g | Protein: 1g | Fiber: 3g

CHAPTER 14: SNACK BAKED TREATS AND PASTRIES

Air Fryer Gluten-Free Coconut Macaroons

Prep: 15 minutes | Cook: 10 minutes | Serves: 8

Ingredients:

- 3 cups shredded coconut, unsweetened (240g)
- 4 large egg whites (120g)
- 1/2 cup granulated sugar (100g)
- 1 tsp vanilla extract (5ml)
- Pinch of salt

Instructions:

1. In a bowl, whisk together egg whites, sugar, vanilla extract, and salt until combined.
2. Fold in shredded coconut.
3. Form small balls of the mixture and place them in the air fryer basket.
4. Cook at 320°F (160°C) for 10 minutes, until golden.
5. Let cool before serving.

Nutrition Facts (Per Serving): Calories: 150 | Fat: 10g | Carbohydrates: 15g | Protein: 2g | Fiber: 3g

Air Fryer Banana Bread with Almond Flour

Prep: 15 minutes | Cook: 30 minutes | Serves: 8

Ingredients:

- 2 ripe bananas, mashed (200g)
- 2 cups almond flour (200g)
- 3 large eggs (150g)
- 1/4 cup honey (60ml)
- 1 tsp baking soda (4g)
- 1/2 tsp salt (2.5g)
- 1 tsp vanilla extract (5ml)

Instructions:

1. In a bowl, combine mashed bananas, eggs, honey, and vanilla extract.
2. Stir in almond flour, baking soda, and salt.
3. Pour batter into a greased loaf pan that fits in the air fryer.
4. Cook at 330°F (165°C) for 30 minutes. Check with a toothpick for doneness.
5. Let cool before slicing.

Nutrition Facts (Per Serving): Calories: 210 | Fat: 14g | Carbohydrates: 18g | Protein: 7g | Fiber: 3g

Air Fryer Light Angel Food Cake

Prep: 20 minutes | Cook: 20 minutes | Serves: 8

Ingredients:

- 1 cup cake flour (120g)
- 1 1/2 cups granulated sugar (300g)
- 12 large egg whites (360g)
- 1 1/2 tsp cream of tartar (6g)
- 1 tsp vanilla extract (5ml)
- Pinch of salt

Instructions:

1. Beat egg whites with cream of tartar and salt until soft peaks form.
2. Gradually add sugar, then vanilla, continuing to beat.
3. Gently fold in sifted cake flour.
4. Pour batter into an ungreased tube pan that fits in the air fryer.
5. Cook at 300°F (150°C) for 20 minutes. Check for doneness.
6. Invert pan to cool the cake completely before removing.

Nutrition Facts (Per Serving): Calories: 210 | Fat: 0g | Carbohydrates: 47g | Protein: 6g | Fiber: 0g

Air Fryer Lemon and Blueberry Muffins

Prep: 15 minutes | Cook: 15 minutes | Serves:6

Ingredients:

- 1 1/2 cups all-purpose flour (180g)
- 1/2 cup granulated sugar (100g)
- 2 tsp baking powder (8g)
- 1/2 tsp salt (2.5g)
- 1/3 cup vegetable oil (80ml)
- 1 large egg (50g)
- 1/3 cup milk (80ml)
- 1 tbsp lemon zest (6g)
- 1 cup blueberries (150g)

Instructions:

1. Mix flour, sugar, baking powder, and salt in a bowl.
2. In another bowl, whisk together oil, egg, milk, and lemon zest.
3. Combine wet and dry ingredients. Fold in blueberries gently.
4. Fill muffin cups in the air fryer basket.
5. Cook at 350°F (177°C) for 15 minutes, or until a toothpick comes out clean.
6. Let cool before serving.

Nutrition Facts (Per Serving): Calories: 280 | Fat: 11g | Carbohydrates: 42g | Protein: 4g | Fiber: 2g

CHAPTER 15: DINNER FISH AND SEAFOOD DELIGHTS

Air Fryer Glazed Mahi Mahi with Mango Salsa and Rice

Prep: 20 minutes | Cook: 15 minutes | Serves: 2

Ingredients:

- 2 Mahi Mahi fillets (150g each)
- 1/4 cup teriyaki sauce (60ml)
- 1 cup cooked rice (190g)
- 1 mango, diced (150g)
- 1/4 red onion, finely chopped (30g)
- Juice of 1 lime
- Salt and pepper to taste

Instructions:

1. Marinate Mahi Mahi fillets in teriyaki sauce for 15 minutes.
2. Mix diced mango, red onion, lime juice, salt, and pepper to make salsa.
3. Air fry Mahi Mahi at 360°F (180°C) for 10-12 minutes.
4. Serve Mahi Mahi over rice with mango salsa on top.

Nutrition Facts (Per Serving): Calories: 380 | Fat: 3g | Carbohydrates: 50g | Protein: 35g | Fiber: 3g

Asian Style Shrimp and Broccoli

Prep: 15 minutes | Cook: 8 minutes | Serves: 4

Ingredients:

- 1 lb shrimp, peeled and detained (450g)
- 2 cups broccoli florets (200g)
- 2 tbsp soy sauce (30ml)
- 1 tbsp sesame oil (15ml)
- 1 tsp ginger, grated (2g)
- 2 cloves garlic, minced (6g)
- 1 tbsp honey (15ml)

Instructions:

1. In a bowl, mix soy sauce, sesame oil, ginger, garlic, and honey.
2. Add shrimp and broccoli, toss to coat.
3. Place in the air fryer basket.
4. Cook at 380°F (193°C) for 8 minutes, shaking halfway through.
5. Serve hot.

Nutrition Facts (Per Serving): Calories: 180 | Fat: 6g | Carbohydrates: 8g | Protein: 24g | Fiber: 2g

Air Fryer Lemon Herb Tilapia with Quinoa Pilaf

Prep: 15 minutes | Cook: 20 minutes | Serves: 2

Ingredients:

- 2 tilapia fillets (150g each)
- Juice and zest of 1 lemon
- 1 tsp dried herbs (thyme, oregano) (2g)
- 1 cup quinoa (170g)
- 2 cups vegetable broth (480ml)
- 1/2 cup diced carrots (60g)
- 1/2 cup peas (75g)
- Salt and pepper to taste

Instructions:

1. Season tilapia with lemon juice, zest, dried herbs, salt, and pepper.
2. Cook quinoa in vegetable broth with carrots and peas until fluffy.
3. Air fry tilapia at 360°F (180°C) for 10 minutes or until cooked through.
4. Serve tilapia over the quinoa pilaf.

Nutrition Facts (Per Serving): Calories: 400 | Fat: 6g | Carbohydrates: 50g | Protein: 35g | Fiber: 6g

Air Fryer Spicy Tuna Patties

Prep: 15 minutes | Cook: 10 minutes | Serves: 4

Ingredients:

- 2 cans tuna in water, drained (340g)
- 1/2 cup breadcrumbs (60g)
- 1 large egg (50g)
- 1/4 cup mayonnaise (60ml)
- 2 tbsp hot sauce (30ml)
- 1/4 cup finely chopped onion (40g)
- 1 tsp garlic powder (3g)
- Salt and pepper to taste

Instructions:

1. In a bowl, mix together tuna, breadcrumbs, egg, mayonnaise, hot sauce, onion, garlic powder, salt, and pepper.
2. Form mixture into patties.
3. Place patties in the air fryer basket.
4. Cook at 375°F (190°C) for 10 minutes, flipping halfway through.
5. Serve hot, optionally with a side of salad or dipping sauce.

Nutrition Facts (Per Serving): Calories: 230 | Fat: 12g | Carbohydrates: 8g | Protein: 20g | Fiber: 1g

Salmon Steaks with Orange and Soy Glaze, Served with Asparagus

Prep: 10 minutes | Marinate: 30 minutes | Cook: 15 minutes | Serves: 2

Ingredients:

- 2 salmon steaks (150g each)
- Salt and pepper to taste
- 1 orange, sliced into rounds
- 2 tbsp soy sauce (30ml)
- 1/2 lb asparagus (225g), trimmed
- 1 tbsp olive oil (15ml)
- 1/2 tsp garlic powder (1g)

Instructions:

1. Season the salmon steaks with salt and pepper.
2. Place the orange slices on top of the salmon and drizzle with soy sauce.
3. Let the salmon marinate for 30 minutes.
4. In the meantime, toss the asparagus with olive oil and garlic powder.
5. Preheat the air fryer to 360°F (180°C).
6. First, air fry the asparagus for 10 minutes, shaking the basket halfway through.
7. Remove the asparagus and keep warm.
8. Place the marinated salmon steaks in the air fryer, laying the orange slices on top.
9. Air fry for about 10 minutes, or until the salmon is cooked through and the orange is slightly caramelized.
10. Serve the salmon steaks with the roasted asparagus on the side.

Nutrition Facts (Per Serving): Calories: 350 | Fat: 20g | Carbohydrates: 15g | Protein: 30g | Fiber: 4g

Air Fryer Sweet and Sour Shrimp

Prep: 15 minutes | Cook: 8 minutes | Serves: 4

Ingredients:

- 1 lb shrimp, peeled and detained (450g)
- 1/2 cup sweet and sour sauce (120ml)
- 1 bell pepper, cut into pieces (150g)
- 1/2 onion, cut into pieces (100g)
- 1 tbsp cornstarch (8g)
- Salt and pepper to taste

Instructions:

1. Toss shrimp with cornstarch, salt, and pepper.
2. Place shrimp, bell pepper, and onion in the air fryer basket.
3. Cook at 380°F (193°C) for 6 minutes.
4. Toss with sweet and sour sauce.
5. Cook for an additional 2 minutes.
6. Serve hot, ideally with rice or noodles.

Nutrition Facts (Per Serving): Calories: 220 | Fat: 2g | Carbohydrates: 18g | Protein: 27g | Fiber: 1g

Air Fryer Sesame Ginger Salmon Packets

Prep: 15 minutes | Cook: 12 minutes | Serves: 2

Ingredients:

- 2 salmon fillets (150g each)
- 2 tbsp soy sauce (30ml)
- 1 tbsp sesame oil (15ml)
- 1 tbsp fresh ginger, grated (6g)
- 1 clove garlic, minced (3g)
- 1 tbsp honey (15ml)
- 1 tsp sesame seeds (2g)
- 2 sheets of aluminum foil

Instructions:

1. In a bowl, whisk together soy sauce, sesame oil, ginger, garlic, and honey.
2. Place each salmon fillet on a sheet of aluminum foil. Pour the marinade over the fillets and sprinkle with sesame seeds.
3. Seal the foil packets and place them in the air fryer basket.
4. Cook at 400°F (204°C) for 12 minutes.
5. Carefully open packets and serve.

Nutrition Facts (Per Serving): Calories: 310 | Fat: 18g | Carbohydrates: 8g | Protein: 30g | Fiber: 0g

Air Fryer Crispy Tilapia Tacos

Prep: 20 minutes | Cook: 10 minutes | Serves: 4

Ingredients:

- 4 tilapia fillets (120g each)
- 1 cup breadcrumbs (120g)
- 1 tsp chili powder (2g)
- 1/2 tsp cumin (1g)
- 1/2 tsp garlic powder (1g)
- 1/2 tsp salt (2.5g)
- 1/4 tsp pepper (1g)
- 8 corn tortillas (200g)
- Toppings: lettuce, tomato, avocado, and lime wedges

Instructions:

1. Mix breadcrumbs with chili powder, cumin, garlic powder, salt, and pepper.
2. Coat tilapia fillets in the breadcrumb mixture.
3. Place in the air fryer basket.
4. Cook at 390°F (199°C) for 10 minutes, flipping halfway through.
5. Serve on corn tortillas with desired toppings.

Nutrition Facts (Per Serving): Calories: 350 | Fat: 6g | Carbohydrates: 45g | Protein: 28g | Fiber: 5g

Air Fryer Stuffed Calamari with Tomato Sauce

Prep: 20 minutes | Cook: 10 minutes | Serves: 2

Ingredients:

- 4 large calamari tubes, cleaned (200g each)
- 1/2 cup breadcrumbs (60g)
- 1/4 cup grated Parmesan cheese (30g)
- 2 cloves garlic, minced (6g)
- 1 tbsp chopped parsley (3g)
- 1 egg, beaten
- Salt and pepper to taste
- 1 cup tomato sauce (240ml)

Instructions:

1. In a bowl, mix breadcrumbs, Parmesan cheese, garlic, parsley, egg, salt, and pepper.
2. Stuff each calamari tube with the breadcrumb mixture.
3. Place stuffed calamari in the air fryer basket.
4. Air fry at 370°F (188°C) for 10 minutes or until calamari is cooked through.
5. Warm the tomato sauce separately and serve with the cooked calamari.

Nutrition Facts (Per Serving): Calories: 350 | Fat: 12g | Carbohydrates: 25g | Protein: 30g | Fiber: 2g

Air Fryer Mini Crab Cakes

Prep: 20 minutes | Cook: 10 minutes | Serves:4

Ingredients:

- 1 lb crab meat, drained and flaked (450g)
- 1/2 cup breadcrumbs (60g)
- 1/4 cup mayonnaise (60ml)
- 1 egg, beaten (50g)
- 2 tbsp green onions, chopped (6g)
- 1 tsp Old Bay seasoning (2g)
- 1 tsp mustard (5ml)
- Salt and pepper to taste
- Lemon wedges for serving

Instructions:

1. In a bowl, mix together crab meat, breadcrumbs, mayonnaise, egg, green onions, Old Bay seasoning, mustard, salt, and pepper.
2. Form the mixture into small patties.
3. Place patties in the air fryer basket.
4. Cook at 375°F (190°C) for 10 minutes, flipping halfway through.
5. Serve hot with lemon wedges.

Nutrition Facts (Per Serving): Calories: 210 | Fat: 10g | Carbohydrates: 8g | Protein: 20g | Fiber: 0.5g

Air Fryer Teriyaki Tuna Steaks with Stir-Fried Veggies

Prep: 15 minutes | Cook: 15 minutes | Serves: 2

Ingredients:

- 2 tuna steaks (150g each)
- 1/4 cup teriyaki sauce (60ml)
- 1 tbsp sesame oil (15ml)
- 1 clove garlic, minced (3g)
- 2 cups mixed vegetables (broccoli, bell pepper, snap peas) (300g)
- 1 tsp ginger, minced (2g)

Instructions:

1. Marinate tuna steaks in teriyaki sauce for 15 minutes.
2. Stir-fry mixed vegetables with sesame oil, ginger, and garlic in the air fryer at 380°F (193°C) for 5 minutes.
3. Add marinated tuna to the air fryer and cook for an additional 10 minutes.
4. Serve tuna steaks with stir-fried vegetables on the side.

Nutrition Facts (Per Serving): Calories: 350 | Fat: 10g | Carbohydrates: 20g | Protein: 40g | Fiber: 5g

Air Fryer Pesto Barramundi with Roasted Cherry Tomatoes

Prep: 10 minutes | Cook: 12 minutes | Serves: 2

Ingredients:

- 2 Barramundi fillets (150g each)
- 2 tbsp pesto sauce (30ml)
- 1 cup cherry tomatoes (150g)
- 1 tbsp olive oil (15ml)
- Salt and pepper to taste

Instructions:

1. Spread pesto sauce over Barramundi fillets.
2. Toss cherry tomatoes in olive oil, salt, and pepper.
3. Air fry Barramundi and cherry tomatoes at 370°F (188°C) for 12 minutes.
4. Serve Barramundi with roasted cherry tomatoes on the side.

Nutrition Facts (Per Serving): Calories: 350 | Fat: 15g | Carbohydrates: 15g | Protein: 40g | Fiber: 2g

CHAPTER 16: FAMILY DINNER FAVORITES

Air Fryer Seafood Paella

Prep: 15 minutes | Cook: 25 minutes | Serves: 4

Ingredients:

- 1 cup Arborio rice (200g)
- 2 cups fish stock (480ml)
- 1/2 lb mixed seafood (shrimp, mussels, squid) (225g)
- 1/2 cup diced tomatoes (90g)
- 1/2 cup frozen peas (75g)
- 1/2 cup bell peppers, chopped (75g)
- 1 tsp paprika (2g)
- 1/2 tsp saffron threads (0.1g)
- Salt and pepper to taste

Instructions:

1. Mix rice, fish stock, paprika, saffron, salt, and pepper in the air fryer basket.
2. Air fry at 360°F (180°C) for 20 minutes.
3. Add mixed seafood, diced tomatoes, peas, and bell peppers.
4. Air fry for an additional 5 minutes or until seafood is cooked.

Nutrition Facts (Per Serving): Calories: 350 | Fat: 6g | Carbohydrates: 50g | Protein: 20g | Fiber: 3g

Air Fryer Seafood and Asparagus Pasta

Prep: 15 minutes | Cook: 15 minutes | Serves: 4

Ingredients:

- 8 oz spaghetti (225g)
- 1/2 lb asparagus, trimmed and cut (225g)
- 1/2 lb shrimp, peeled and deveined (225g)
- 2 tbsp olive oil (30ml)
- 2 cloves garlic, minced (6g)
- Salt and pepper to taste
- Parmesan cheese for serving (optional)

Instructions:

1. Cook spaghetti as per package instructions.
2. Toss asparagus and shrimp with olive oil, garlic, salt, and pepper.
3. Air fry at 390°F (200°C) for 10 minutes.
4. Toss cooked pasta with air-fried asparagus and shrimp.
5. Serve with Parmesan cheese.

Nutrition Facts (Per Serving): Calories: 400 | Fat: 12g | Carbohydrates: 50g | Protein: 25g | Fiber: 3g

Air Fryer Mediterranean Stuffed Sardines

Prep: 20 minutes | Cook: 10 minutes | Serves: 4

Ingredients:

- 8 fresh sardines, cleaned and gutted (400g total)
- 1/4 cup breadcrumbs (30g)
- 2 tbsp chopped fresh parsley (6g)
- 2 cloves garlic, minced (6g)
- 2 tbsp olive oil (30ml), plus extra for brushing
- 1 tbsp lemon juice (15ml)
- 1/2 tsp salt (2.5g)
- 1/4 tsp pepper (1g)
- 1/4 cup chopped olives (30g)
- 1/4 cup diced feta cheese (30g)

Instructions:

1. In a bowl, mix breadcrumbs, parsley, garlic, 1 tbsp olive oil, lemon juice, salt, pepper, olives, and feta cheese.
2. Open each sardine and stuff with the breadcrumb mixture.
3. Brush the stuffed sardines with olive oil.
4. Place sardines in the air fryer basket in a single layer.
5. Cook at 400°F (204°C) for 10 minutes, until cooked through and crispy.
6. Serve with a side of mixed greens or a fresh salad.

Nutrition Facts (Per Serving): Calories: 190 | Fat: 11g | Carbohydrates: 6g | Protein: 17g | Fiber: 1g

Air Fryer Pasta with Mushrooms and Cheese

Prep: 10 minutes | Cook: 20 minutes | Serves: 2

Ingredients:

- 8 oz whole wheat pasta (225g)
- 1 cup sliced mushrooms (70g)
- 2 cloves garlic, minced (6g)
- 1 tbsp olive oil (15ml)
- 1/2 cup grated Parmesan cheese (50g)
- Salt and pepper to taste
- Fresh parsley, chopped, for garnish

Instructions:

1. Cook pasta according to package instructions. Drain and set aside.
2. In the air fryer, toss mushrooms and garlic with olive oil, salt, and pepper.
3. Air fry at 360°F (180°C) for 10 minutes, until mushrooms are tender.
4. In a serving bowl, combine cooked pasta with air-fried mushrooms.
5. Sprinkle with Parmesan cheese and toss well.
6. Garnish with fresh parsley before serving.

Nutrition Facts (Per Serving): Calories: 400 | Fat: 15g | Carbohydrates: 50g | Protein: 20g | Fiber: 8g

Herb-Marinated Anchovies with Roasted Peppers and Baby Greens in Air Fryer

Prep: 10 minutes | Cook: 10 minutes | Serves: 2

Ingredients:

- 1 cup anchovies, cleaned (150g)
- 1/4 cup mixed fresh herbs (parsley, dill, cilantro) finely chopped (15g)
- 2 tbsp olive oil (30ml)
- 1 bell pepper, sliced (120g)
- 2 cups baby greens (spinach, arugula) (60g)
- 1 tbsp lemon juice (15ml)
- 1 clove garlic, minced (3g)
- Salt and pepper to taste

Instructions:

1. In a bowl, mix anchovies with half of the olive oil, lemon juice, minced garlic, fresh herbs, salt, and pepper. Let marinate for 10 minutes.
2. Toss bell pepper slices with remaining olive oil, salt, and pepper.
3. Place bell pepper in the air fryer basket and cook at 380°F (193°C) for 5 minutes.
4. Add marinated anchovies to the air fryer and cook for another 5 minutes.
5. Serve the anchovies and roasted peppers over a bed of baby greens.

Nutrition Facts (Per Serving): Calories: 350 | Fat: 20g | Carbohydrates: 10g | Protein: 30g | Fiber: 2g

Air Fryer Calamari Rings with Mediterranean Vegetables

Prep: 15 minutes | Cook: 20 minutes | Serves: 2

Ingredients:

- 1 lb calamari rings, fresh or thawed (450g)
- 1 zucchini, sliced (200g)
- 1 red bell pepper, sliced (120g)
- 1 yellow bell pepper, sliced (120g)
- 1 red onion, sliced (100g)
- 2 tbsp olive oil (30ml)
- 1 tsp dried oregano (1g)
- 1/2 tsp garlic powder (1g)
- Salt and pepper to taste
- Lemon wedges for serving

Instructions:

1. In a bowl, toss calamari rings with 1 tbsp olive oil, garlic powder, and a pinch of salt and pepper.
2. In another bowl, mix zucchini, bell peppers, red onion, remaining olive oil, oregano, salt, and pepper.
3. Place the vegetables in the air fryer basket and cook at 380°F (193°C) for 10 minutes.
4. Add calamari rings to the basket and cook for another 10 minutes, until calamari is cooked and vegetables are tender.
5. Serve calamari rings and vegetables with lemon wedges on the side.

Nutrition Facts (Per Serving): Calories: 350 | Fat: 15g | Carbohydrates: 25g | Protein: 30g | Fiber: 3g

Air Fryer Cajun Spiced Catfish with Quinoa Salad

Prep: 15 minutes | Cook: 20 minutes | Serves: 2

Ingredients:

For Catfish:
- 2 catfish fillets (200g each)
- 1 tbsp Cajun seasoning (6g)
- 1/2 tsp garlic powder (1g)
- 1/2 tsp onion powder (1g)
- Salt and pepper to taste
- 1 tbsp olive oil (15ml)

For Quinoa Salad:
- 1/2 cup quinoa (85g), rinsed
- 1 cup water (240ml)
- 1 small cucumber, diced (150g)
- 1/2 red bell pepper, diced (75g)
- 1/4 red onion, finely chopped (30g)
- 2 tbsp lemon juice (30ml)
- 2 tbsp olive oil (30ml)
- Salt and pepper to taste
- Fresh parsley, chopped, for garnish

Instructions:

For the Catfish:

1. Mix Cajun seasoning, garlic powder, onion powder, salt, and pepper.
2. Rub the spice mixture on both sides of the catfish fillets.
3. Drizzle fillets with olive oil.
4. Place fillets in the air fryer basket.
5. Cook at 400°F (204°C) for 10 minutes, flipping halfway through.

For the Quinoa Salad:

1. In a saucepan, combine quinoa and water. Bring to a boil, then reduce heat and simmer for 15 minutes, or until water is absorbed.
2. Fluff the cooked quinoa with a fork and let it cool.
3. In a large bowl, combine cooled quinoa, cucumber, red bell pepper, and red onion.
4. In a small bowl, whisk together lemon juice, olive oil, salt, and pepper. Pour over the quinoa salad and mix well.
5. Garnish with fresh parsley.
6. Serve the hot Cajun spiced catfish with the refreshing quinoa salad on the side.

Nutrition Facts (Per Serving): Calories: 390 | Fat: 20g | Carbohydrates: 30g | Protein: 28g | Fiber: 4g

CHAPTER 17: DINNER ELEGANT MEALS FOR SPECIAL OCCASIONS

Air Fryer Garlic Shrimp Skewers

Prep: 10 minutes | Cook: 6 minutes | Serves: 4

Ingredients:

- 1 lb large shrimp, peeled and detained (450g)
- 3 cloves garlic, minced (9g)
- 2 tbsp olive oil (30ml)
- 1 tbsp lemon juice (15ml)
- 1/2 tsp paprika (1g)
- 1/2 tsp salt (2.5g)
- 1/4 tsp pepper (1g)
- 8 wooden skewers, soaked in water

Instructions:

1. Marinate shrimp with garlic, olive oil, lemon juice, paprika, salt, and pepper for 30 minutes.
2. Thread shrimp onto soaked skewers.
3. Place skewers in the air fryer basket.
4. Cook at 400°F (204°C) for 6 minutes, flipping halfway through.
5. Serve hot.

Nutrition Facts (Per Serving): Calories: 180 | Fat: 8g | Carbohydrates: 1g | Protein: 24g | Fiber: 0g

Air Fryer Mini Fish Cakes

Prep: 20 minutes | Cook: 10 minutes | Serves: 4

Ingredients:

- 1 lb white fish fillets, cooked and flaked (450g)
- 1/2 cup breadcrumbs (60g)
- 1 egg (50g)
- 1/4 cup chopped parsley (6g)
- 1 tsp lemon zest (2g)
- Salt and pepper to taste
- 1/4 cup all-purpose flour for coating (30g)

Instructions:

1. Mix flaked fish, breadcrumbs, egg, parsley, lemon zest, salt, and pepper.
2. Form mixture into small patties.
3. Lightly coat each patty in flour.
4. Place in the air fryer basket.
5. Cook at 375°F (190°C) for 10 minutes, flipping halfway through.
6. Serve with tartar sauce or lemon wedges.

Nutrition Facts (Per Serving): Calories: 220 | Fat: 4g | Carbohydrates: 12g | Protein: 35g | Fiber: 1g

Air Fryer Herb Crusted Halibut with Lemon Butter Green Beans

Prep: 10 minutes | Cook: 12 minutes | Serves: 2

Ingredients:

- 2 halibut fillets (150g each)
- 1 tbsp mixed dried herbs (parsley, thyme, dill) (3g)
- 1/2 lemon, zest and juice
- 2 cups green beans, trimmed (200g)
- 1 tbsp butter, melted (15ml)
- Salt and pepper to taste

Instructions:

1. Season halibut with mixed herbs, lemon zest, salt, and pepper.
2. Toss green beans with lemon juice, melted butter, salt, and pepper.
3. Place halibut and green beans in the air fryer basket.
4. Air fry at 360°F (180°C) for 12 minutes, until the fish is flaky and green beans are tender.
5. Serve halibut with lemon butter green beans on the side.

Nutrition Facts (Per Serving): Calories: 350 | Fat: 12g | Carbohydrates: 10g | Protein: 40g | Fiber: 4g

Salmon and Asparagus Bundles

Prep: 10 minutes | Cook: 10 minutes | Serves: 4

Ingredients:

- 4 salmon fillets (150g each)
- 16 asparagus spears, trimmed (200g)
- 2 tbsp olive oil (30ml)
- 1 tbsp lemon juice (15ml)
- Salt and pepper to taste
- 4 lemon slices for garnish

Instructions:

1. Brush salmon fillets and asparagus with olive oil.
2. Season with salt, pepper, and lemon juice.
3. Divide asparagus into four bundles. Wrap each bundle with a salmon fillet.
3. Place bundles in the air fryer basket.
4. Cook at 400°F (204°C) for 10 minutes or until salmon is cooked through.
5. Serve with a lemon slice on top.

Nutrition Facts (Per Serving): Calories: 230 | Fat: 13g | Carbohydrates: 2g | Protein: 25g | Fiber: 1g

Air Fryer Flounder with Spinach and Roasted Cherry Tomatoes

Prep: 10 minutes | **Cook:** 15 minutes | **Serves:** 2

Ingredients:

- 2 flounder fillets (150g each)
- 2 cups fresh spinach (60g)
- 1 cup cherry tomatoes (150g)
- 1 tbsp olive oil (15ml)
- 1 clove garlic, minced (3g)
- Salt and pepper to taste

Instructions:

1. Season flounder with salt and pepper.
2. Toss cherry tomatoes with half the olive oil, salt, and pepper.
3. Air fry tomatoes at 380°F (193°C) for 10 minutes. In the meantime, sauté spinach with garlic and remaining olive oil until wilted.
4. Add flounder to the air fryer and cook for an additional 5 minutes.
5. Serve flounder with sautéed spinach and roasted cherry tomatoes.

Nutrition Facts (Per Serving): Calories: 380 | Fat: 15g | Carbohydrates: 12g | Protein: 40g | Fiber: 3g

Air Fryer Teriyaki Eel Steaks with Stir-Fried Bok Choy

Prep: 10 minutes | **Cook:** 15 minutes | **Serves:** 2

Ingredients:

- 2 eel steaks (150g each)
- 1/4 cup teriyaki sauce (60ml)
- 2 cups bok choy, chopped (170g)
- 1 tbsp sesame oil (15ml)
- 1 clove garlic, minced (3g)
- 1 tsp ginger, minced (2g)
- 1 tbsp soy sauce (15ml)
- Salt and pepper to taste
- Sesame seeds for garnish (optional)

Instructions:

1. Marinate eel steaks in teriyaki sauce for 10 minutes.
2. In a bowl, mix sesame oil, garlic, ginger, and soy sauce. Toss bok choy in this mixture.
3. Air fry eel steaks at 380°F (193°C) for 10 minutes, flipping halfway through.
4. Remove eel and keep warm. In the same air fryer, cook bok choy for 5 minutes until wilted.
5. Serve teriyaki eel steaks with stir-fried bok choy and sprinkle sesame seeds on top.

Nutrition Facts (Per Serving): Calories: 350 | Fat: 15g | Carbohydrates: 15g | Protein: 35g | Fiber: 2g

CHAPTER 18: DINNER VEGETARIAN AND VEGAN ADAPTATIONS

Air Fryer Mediterranean Veggie Kebabs

Prep: 15 minutes | Cook: 10 minutes | Serves: 4

Ingredients:

- 1 zucchini, sliced (200g)
- 1 bell pepper, cut into pieces (150g)
- 1 red onion, cut into wedges (100g)
- 8 cherry tomatoes (80g)
- 8 mushrooms (100g)
- 2 tbsp olive oil (30ml)
- 1 tsp dried oregano (5g)
- Salt and pepper to taste
- 4 wooden skewers, soaked in water

Instructions:

1. Thread zucchini, bell pepper, red onion, cherry tomatoes, and mushrooms onto skewers.
2. Brush with olive oil and sprinkle with oregano, salt, and pepper.
3. Cook in air fryer at 400°F for 10 minutes, turning halfway through.

Nutrition Facts (Per Serving): Calories: 110 | Fat: 7g | Carbohydrates: 10g | Protein: 2g | Fiber: 2g

Crispy Tofu and Broccoli Bowls

Prep: 15 minutes | Cook: 20 minutes | Serves: 4

Ingredients:

- 14 oz firm tofu, pressed and cubed (400g)
- 1 head of broccoli, cut into florets (300g)
- 2 tbsp soy sauce (30ml)
- Sesame seeds for garnish
- 1 tbsp sesame oil (15ml)
- 2 tbsp cornstarch (30g)
- 2 cups cooked brown rice (370g)

Instructions:

1. Toss tofu with soy sauce, sesame oil, and cornstarch.
2. Cook tofu and broccoli in air fryer at 380°F for 20 minutes, shaking basket halfway through.
3. Serve over brown rice and garnish with sesame seeds.

Nutrition Facts (Per Serving): Calories: 320 | Fat: 12g | Carbohydrates: 40g | Protein: 15g | Fiber: 5g

Air Fryer Thai Red Curry with Vegetables

Prep: 15 minutes | Cook: 15 minutes | Serves: 4

Ingredients:

- 1 tbsp coconut oil (15ml)
- 1/4 cup Thai red curry paste (60ml)
- 1 can coconut milk (400ml)
- 1 bell pepper, sliced (150g)
- 1 zucchini, sliced (200g)
- Fresh basil leaves for garnish
- 1 cup snap peas (100g)
- 1/2 cup bamboo shoots (75g)
- 1 tbsp fish sauce (15ml)
- 1 tsp brown sugar (5g)
- 2 cups cooked jasmine rice (370g)

Instructions:

1. Heat coconut oil in a pan, add red curry paste, and fry for 1 minute.
2. Stir in coconut milk, vegetables, fish sauce, and brown sugar. Cook until vegetables are tender.
3. Serve the curry over jasmine rice and garnish with fresh basil.

Nutrition Facts (Per Serving): Calories: 420 | Fat: 22g | Carbohydrates: 48g | Protein: 8g | Fiber: 3g

Air Fryer Greek Style Stuffed Eggplant

Prep: 20 minutes | Cook: 15 minutes | Serves:4

Ingredients:

- 2 large eggplants, halved lengthwise (500g each)
- 2 tbsp olive oil (30ml)
- 1 small onion, finely chopped (100g)
- 2 cloves garlic, minced
- 1 tomato, diced (100g)
- 1/2 cup crumbled feta cheese (75g)
- 2 tbsp chopped fresh parsley (10g)
- Salt and pepper to taste

Instructions:

1. Scoop out the center of the eggplant halves, leaving a thin shell. Chop the scooped flesh.
2. Sauté onion, garlic, and chopped eggplant in olive oil until soft. Add tomato and cook for 2 minutes.
3. Stir in feta cheese, parsley, salt, and pepper.
4. Stuff eggplant shells with the mixture. Cook in air fryer at 360°F for 15 minutes.

Nutrition Facts (Per Serving): Calories: 180 | Fat: 10g | Carbohydrates: 20g | Protein: 5g | Fiber: 7g

CHAPTER 19: BONUSES

Meal Plans and Shopping Templates: Tailor-made for Air Fryer Enthusiasts.

Embark on a flavorful journey with our 30-day Air Fryer meal plan, meticulously crafted to enhance your culinary experience. This shopping template is your gateway to effortless meal preparation, emphasizing the charm of air fryer cooking. It prioritizes fresh, wholesome ingredients, steering clear of overly processed foods and unnecessary additives.

As you navigate through the aisles, be vigilant of hidden sugars and unwanted additives, particularly in premade sauces and dressings. Our air fryer recipes champion the use of fresh, whole foods, bringing out their natural flavors and textures in a healthier way. Adjust quantities to suit your household's needs and dietary preferences. Happy air frying and enjoy savoring every flavorful, healthy meal!

Grocery Shopping List for 7-Day Meal Plan

Proteins

Eggs (for Air Fryer Veggie Frittata, Spinach and Feta Air Fryer Omelette, etc.)
Mahi Mahi (for Air Fryer Glazed Mahi Mahi with Mango Salsa and Rice)
Salmon (for Air Fryer Mediterranean Stuffed Sardines)
Chicken (for Air Fryer Quinoa-Stuffed Tomatoes, Asian Style Shrimp and Broccoli)
Shrimp (for Air Fryer Seafood Paella)
Halibut (for Air Fryer Herb Crusted Halibut with Lemon Butter Green Beans)
Tilapia (for Air Fryer Lemon Herb Tilapia with Quinoa Pilaf)

Dairy and Dairy Alternatives:

Feta Cheese (for Spinach and Feta Air Fryer Omelette, Air Fryer Greek Style Zucchini Fritters)
Milk or Almond Milk (for Almond Flour Blueberry Pancakes, Gluten-Free Almond Butter Waffles)
Greek Yogurt (for Air Fryer Mini Breakfast Quiches)
Butter (for various recipes)

Fruits:

Bananas (for Air Fryer Banana Nut Oatmeal Muffins)
Mango (for Air Fryer Glazed Mahi Mahi with Mango Salsa and Rice)
Apples (for Air Fryer Baked Apples with Cinnamon)
Berries (for Gluten-Free Almond Butter Waffles with Berries, Air Fryer Dark Chocolate Dipped Strawberries)
Lemons (for Air Fryer Lemon Herb Tilapia with Quinoa Pilaf, Air Fryer Herb Crusted Halibut)

Vegetables & Herbs:

Mixed Greens (for Air Fryer Mediterranean Chickpea Salad, Air Fryer Seafood Paella)
Cauliflower (for Air Fryer Buffalo Cauliflower Bites, Air Fryer Cauliflower Steak Pitas)
Zucchini (for Air Fryer Zucchini Chips, Air Fryer Greek Style Zucchini Fritters)
Tomatoes (for Air Fryer Quinoa-Stuffed Tomatoes, Air Fryer Stuffed Portabello Mushrooms)
Spinach (for Spinach and Feta Air Fryer Omelette, Air Fryer Flounder with Spinach and Roasted Cherry Tomatoes)
Asparagus (for Air Fryer Asparagus and Prosciutto Egg Cups)

Fresh Herbs (parsley, basil, dill, etc. for flavoring)

Grains & Bakery:

Quinoa (for Air Fryer Lemon Herb Tilapia with Quinoa Pilaf)
Almond Flour (for Almond Flour Blueberry Pancakes, Air Fryer Banana Bread with Almond Flour)
Oatmeal (for Air Fryer Banana Nut Oatmeal Muffins)

Nuts & Seeds:

Nuts for Air Fryer Banana Nut Oatmeal Muffins
Almond Butter (for Gluten-Free Almond Butter Waffles with Berries)

Pantry Staples:

Olive Oil (for cooking)
Various Spices (salt, pepper, paprika, etc.)
Balsamic Vinegar or other dressings (for salads)
Soy Sauce (for Asian Style Shrimp and Broccoli)
Baking Ingredients (baking powder, vanilla extract, etc.)

Miscellaneous:

Dark Chocolate (for Air Fryer Dark Chocolate Dipped Strawberries)
Cocoa Powder (for Air Fryer Vegan Chocolate Avocado Cake)
Sugar-Free Sweeteners (if required for desserts)

Grocery Shopping List for 8-14 Day Meal Plan

Proteins

Tuna (for Air Fryer Spicy Tuna Patties, Air Fryer Teriyaki Tuna Steaks)
Salmon (for Smoked Salmon and Dill Breakfast Bites, Air Fryer Sesame Ginger Salmon Packets)
Chicken Breast (for Air Fryer Chicken Fajita Bowls)
Pork Steaks (for Air Fryer Pork Steaks with Roasted Broccoli and Carrots)
Ground Beef (for Air Fryer Beef Goulash with Vegetables)
Crab Meat (for Air Fryer Mini Crab Cakes)
Turkey (for Turkey and Avocado Air Fryer Wraps)

Dairy and Dairy Alternatives:

Cheese (for Air Fryer Mini Cheese and Ham Quesadillas, Air Fryer Berry Breakfast Pitas)
Milk or Milk Alternatives (for Air Fryer Blueberry Breakfast Scones, Air Fryer Apple Cinnamon Oatmeal Cups)
Butter (for various recipes)
Greek Yogurt (for Air Fryer Berry Breakfast Pitas, Air Fryer Lemon and Blueberry Muffins)

Fruits:

Blueberries (for Air Fryer Blueberry Breakfast Scones, Air Fryer Lemon and Blueberry Muffins)
Apples (for Crispy Air Fryer Hash Browns, Spiced Apple Air Fryer Turnovers)
Pineapple (for Air Fryer Honey Glazed Pineapple Slices)
Bananas (for Air Fryer Banana Bread with Almond Flour)
Oranges (for Salmon Steaks with Orange and Soy Glaze)

Vegetables & Herbs:

Mixed Vegetables (for Air Fryer Roasted Veggie Quinoa Salad, Air Fryer Beef Goulash with Vegetables)
Broccoli and Carrots (for Air Fryer Pork Steaks with Roasted Broccoli and Carrots)
Lettuce, Tomatoes, Avocado (for Turkey and Avocado Air Fryer Wraps)
Zucchini, Eggplant, Bell Peppers (for Air Fryer Veggie-Stuffed Pita Pockets)
Asparagus (for Salmon Steaks with Orange and Soy Glaze)
Fresh Herbs (dill, parsley, basil, etc. for flavoring)

Grains & Bakery:

Quinoa (for Air Fryer Roasted Veggie Quinoa Salad)
Whole Grain or Almond Flour (for Air Fryer Blueberry Breakfast Scones, Air Fryer Apple Cinnamon Oatmeal Cups)
Tortillas or Pita Bread (for Air Fryer Mini Cheese and Ham Quesadillas, Air Fryer Veggie-Stuffed Pita Pockets)

Nuts & Seeds:

Almonds or Almond Flour

Pantry Staples:

Olive Oil (for cooking)
Various Spices (salt, pepper, garlic powder, etc.)
Soy Sauce (for Salmon Steaks with Orange and Soy Glaze, Air Fryer Teriyaki Tuna Steaks)
Balsamic Vinegar or other dressings (for salads)
Baking Ingredients (baking powder, vanilla extract, etc.)

Miscellaneous:

Coconut (for Air Fryer Gluten-Free Coconut Macaroons)
Dark Chocolate (if needed for desserts)
Honey (for Air Fryer Honey Glazed Pineapple Slices)
Matcha Powder (for Air Fryer Matcha Green Tea Mochi)

Grocery Shopping List for 15-21 Day Meal Plan

Proteins:

Sausage (for Air Fryer Breakfast Sausage Patties)
Chicken Breast (for Chicken Caesar Salad Pita Pockets, Air Fryer Lemon-Herb Chicken Breast)
Barramundi (for Air Fryer Pesto Barramundi with Roasted Cherry Tomatoes)
Anchovies (for Herb-Marinated Anchovies with Roasted Peppers and Baby Greens)
Turkey (for Air Fryer Turkey and Spinach Meatballs)
Pork Steaks (for Air Fryer Pork Steaks with Roasted Broccoli and Carrots)
Catfish (for Air Fryer Cajun Spiced Catfish with Quinoa Salad)
Shrimp (for Air Fryer Garlic Shrimp Skewers)

Dairy and Dairy Alternatives:

Eggs (for Air Fryer Asparagus and Prosciutto Egg Cups, Air Fryer Egg and Vegetable Muffins)
Cheese (for Air Fryer Banana Pepper and Cheese Bagel, Air Fryer Brie and Cranberry Bites)
Brie Cheese (for Air Fryer Brie and Cranberry Bites)
Milk or Milk Alternatives (for various recipes)

Fruits:

Bananas (for Air Fryer Banana Pepper and Cheese Bagel)
Avocado (for Air Fryer Vegan Chocolate Avocado Cake)
Pears (for Air Fryer Pear and Granola Parfaits)
Strawberries (for Air Fryer Dark Chocolate Dipped Strawberries)

Vegetables & Herbs:

Asparagus (for Air Fryer Asparagus and Prosciutto Egg Cups, Air Fryer Seafood and Asparagus Pasta)
Mixed Vegetables (for Air Fryer Lemon-Herb Chicken Breast with Vegetables, Air Fryer Calamari Rings with Mediterranean Vegetables)
Bell Peppers (for Mediterranean Stuffed Bell Peppers)
Zucchini, Corn (for Air Fryer Zucchini and Corn Fritters)
Broccoli and Carrots (for Air Fryer Pork Steaks with Roasted Broccoli and Carrots)
Baby Greens (for Herb-Marinated Anchovies with Roasted Peppers and Baby Greens)
Fresh Herbs (for various recipes, including pesto)

Grains & Bakery:

Bagels (for Air Fryer Banana Pepper and Cheese Bagel)
Quinoa (for Air Fryer Cajun Spiced Catfish with Quinoa Salad)
Whole Grain or Corn Tortillas (for Air Fryer Veggie Breakfast Tacos, Air Fryer Rainbow Veggie Pockets)
Pasta (for Air Fryer Seafood and Asparagus Pasta)

Nuts & Seeds:

Nuts and Seeds (for Air Fryer Pear and Granola Parfaits)

Pantry Staples:

Olive Oil (for cooking)
Various Spices (salt, pepper, garlic powder, Cajun spices, etc.)
Coconut (for Air Fryer Gluten-Free Coconut Macaroons)
Matcha Powder (for Air Fryer Matcha Green Tea Mochi)
Baking Ingredients (baking powder, vanilla extract, etc.)
Miscellaneous:

Dark Chocolate (for Air Fryer Dark Chocolate Dipped Strawberries)
Cocoa Powder (for Air Fryer Vegan Chocolate Avocado Cake)
Honey (for various recipes)

Grocery Shopping List for 22-28 Day Meal Plan

Proteins:

Pork Tenderloin (for Air Fryer Herded Pork Tenderloin with Vegetables)
Halibut (for Air Fryer Herb Crusted Halibut with Lemon Butter Green Beans)
Chicken Breast (for Air Fryer Chicken Fajita Bowls)
Salmon (for Salmon and Asparagus Bundles)
Flounder (for Air Fryer Flounder with Spinach and Roasted Cherry Tomatoes)
Eel (for Air Fryer Teriyaki Eel Steaks with Stir-Fried Bok Choy)
Tofu (for Crispy Tofu and Broccoli Bowls)
Turkey (for Turkey and Avocado Air Fryer Wraps)

Dairy and Dairy Alternatives:

Eggs (for Spinach and Feta Air Fryer Omelette, Air Fryer Mini Breakfast Quiches)
Feta Cheese (for Spinach and Feta Air Fryer Omelette)
Cheese (for Air Fryer Mini Cheese and Ham Quesadillas, Air Fryer Veggie-Stuffed Pita Pockets)
Milk or Milk Alternatives (for Air Fryer Banana Nut Oatmeal Muffins, Air Fryer Breakfast Pizza)
Brie Cheese (for Air Fryer Brie and Cranberry Bites)

Fruits:

Bananas (for Air Fryer Banana Nut Oatmeal Muffins)
Apples (for Air Fryer Baked Apples with Cinnamon)
Oranges (for Air Fryer Flourless Orange Chocolate Cake)

Vegetables & Herbs:

Green Beans (for Air Fryer Herb Crusted Halibut with Lemon Butter Green Beans)
Mixed Vegetables (for Air Fryer Herded Pork Tenderloin with Vegetables, Air Fryer Beef Goulash with Vegetables)
Spinach (for Air Fryer Flounder with Spinach and Roasted Cherry Tomatoes, Air Fryer Veggie Frittata)
Eggplant (for Air Fryer Cumin-Spiced Eggplant Slices with Tahini Sauce)
Bok Choy (for Air Fryer Teriyaki Eel Steaks with Stir-Fried Bok Choy)
Asparagus (for Prosciutto-Wrapped Asparagus, Salmon and Asparagus Bundles)
Fresh Herbs (parsley, basil, etc. for flavoring)

Grains & Bakery:

Oats (for Air Fryer Granola Clusters)
Tortillas or Pita Bread (for Air Fryer Mini Cheese and Ham Quesadillas, Air Fryer Veggie-Stuffed Pita Pockets, Low-Carb Air Fryer Burritos)
Whole Grain or Almond Flour (for Air Fryer Banana Nut Oatmeal Muffins, Air Fryer Breakfast Pizza)

Nuts & Seeds:

Nuts (for Air Fryer Granola Clusters, Air Fryer Banana Nut Oatmeal Muffins)

Pantry Staples:

Olive Oil (for cooking)
Various Spices (salt, pepper, garlic powder, etc.)
Tahini (for Air Fryer Cumin-Spiced Eggplant Slices with Tahini Sauce)
Soy Sauce (for Air Fryer Teriyaki Eel Steaks with Stir-Fried Bok Choy)
Coconut (for Air Fryer Flourless Orange Chocolate Cake)
Baking Ingredients (baking powder, vanilla extract, etc.)

Miscellaneous:

Cocoa Powder (for Air Fryer Flourless Orange Chocolate Cake)
Dark Chocolate (if needed for desserts)
Honey (for various recipes)

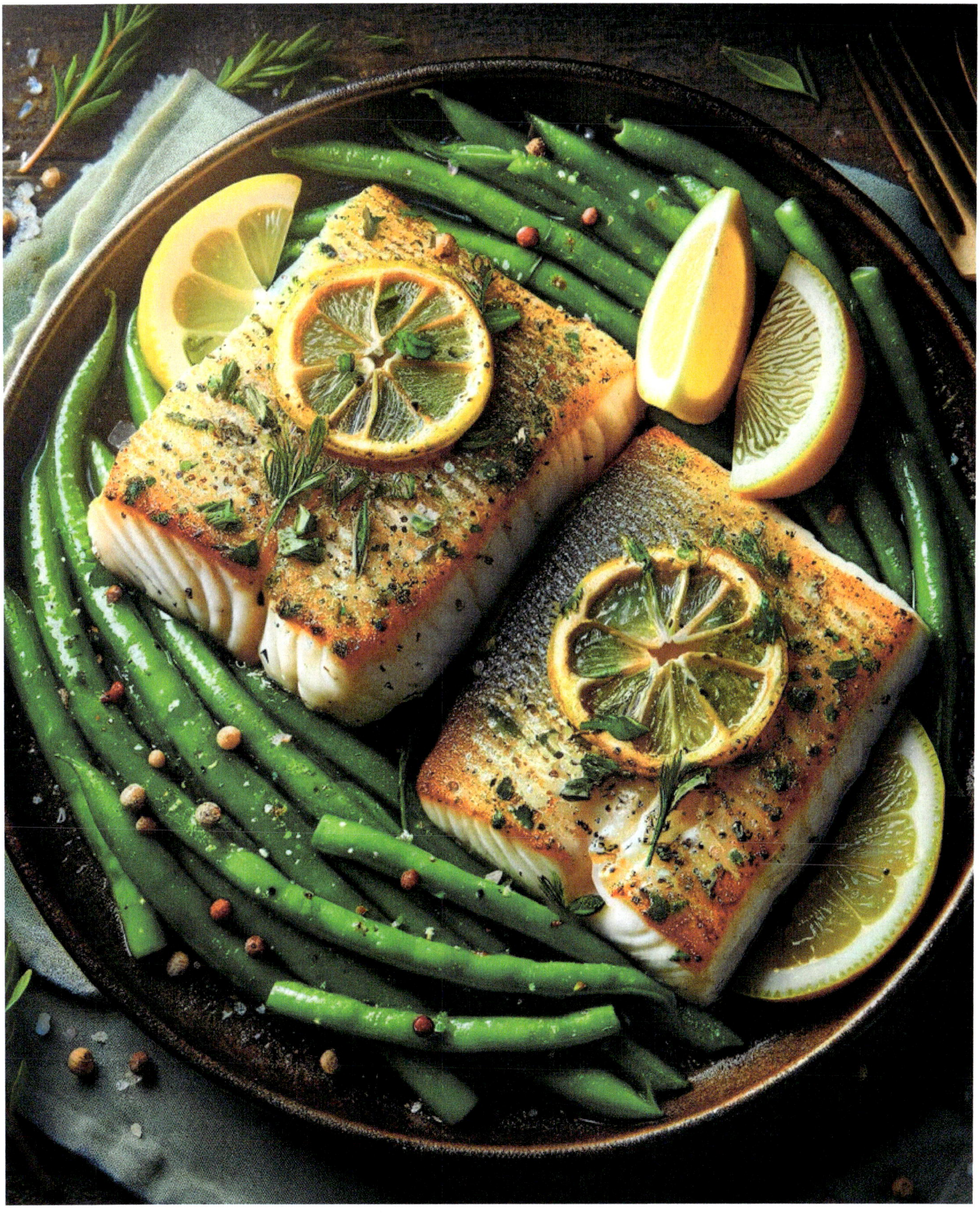

Printed in Great Britain
by Amazon